YAZOO

JUNIOR
A

Companion

T0350584

PEARSON
Longman

Tammy Alexiou

Αγαπητοί γονείς και παιδιά,

Το βιβλίο που κρατάτε στα χέρια σας είναι ένα χρήσιμο βοήθημα για τις λέξεις και τη γραμματική που θα συναντήσετε μέσα στο **YAZOO** A Pupils' Book.

Κάθε μάθημα ξεκινάει με την παρουσίαση των αγγλικών λέξεων στα Ελληνικά με τη σειρά που αυτές εμφανίζονται μέσα στο Pupils' Book. Στη συνέχεια ο Tag σας εξηγεί με απλά λόγια και παραδείγματα τη γραμματική, ώστε να την καταλάβετε εύκολα και γρήγορα! Το μάθημα ολοκληρώνεται με τις ασκήσεις που θα σας βοηθήσουν να κάνετε περισσότερη εξάσκηση σε αυτά που έχετε ήδη μάθει. Οι ασκήσεις αυτές δεν είναι πάντα ίδιες, αλλά είναι πάντα εύκολες!

Το βιβλίο αυτό είναι καλύτερο να το χρησιμοποιείτε στο σπίτι. Έτσι, όταν θέλετε να προετοιμαστείτε για το μάθημα των Αγγλικών, ανοίγετε και το Pupils' Book και το Companion στο μάθημα που έχετε καλύψει. Διαβάζετε την ιστορία στο Pupils' Book και μετά διαβάζετε τις λέξεις στο Companion για να θυμηθείτε τι σημαίνουν. Έπειτα διαβάζετε τη γραμματική και τα παραδείγματα για να κάνετε επανάληψη αυτά που μάθατε στην τάξη. Αφήνετε για το τέλος τις ασκήσεις για να δείτε πόσο καλά τα θυμάστε!

Αν ξεχάστε πώς προφέρεται μία λέξη, δεν πειράζει! Μπορείτε να γυρίσετε στις τελευταίες σελίδες του Companion και να δείτε πώς διαβάζονται. Σε αυτό το σημείο, εσείς οι γονείς πρέπει να θυμάστε πως είναι καλύτερο τα παιδιά να ακούνε τη δασκάλα τους ή το CD για τη σωστή προφορά των λέξεων, γιατί συχνά προσπαθούμε να προφέρουμε μία αγγλική λέξη με ελληνικό τρόπο και τα παιδιά την ακούνε και τη μαθαίνουν λάθος.

Ελπίζουμε το βιβλίο αυτό να σας φανεί χρήσιμο, αλλά κυρίως ευχάριστο, γιατί το πιο σημαντικό τώρα που αποκτάτε μεγαλύτερη επαφή με τα Αγγλικά είναι να διασκεδάζετε μαθαίνοντας!

Καλή περιπλάνηση και καλή διασκέδαση στον κόσμο του **YAZOO**!

Θωμαή Αλεξίου

Contents

Instructions
Οδηγίες

Answer. Απάντησε.

Ask. Ρώτησε.

Ask your friend.

Ρώτησε το φίλο σου/τη φίλη σου.

Chant. Τραγούδησε ρυθμικά.

Choose. Διάλεξε.

Circle. Κύκλωσε.

Colour. Χρωμάτισε.

Complete. Συμπλήρωσε.

Correct the wrong sentences.

Διόρθωσε τις λάθος προτάσεις.

Count. Μέτρησε.

Do. Κάνε.

Do the crossword. Λύσε το σταυρόλεξο.

Draw. Ζωγράφισε.

Draw yourself.

Ζωγράφισε τον εαυτό σου.

Find. Βρες.

Find the differences and write.

Βρες τις διαφορές και γράψε.

Find the odd one out.

Βρες το διαφορετικό.

Find the secret word.

Βρες τη μυστική λέξη.

Join. Ένωσε.

Label. Δώσε ένα όνομα.

Listen. Άκουσε.

Look. Κοίταξε.

Make. Φτιάξε.

Match. Ταίριαξε.

Number. Αρίθμησε.

Number in order.

Αρίθμησε με τη σειρά.

Play the game. Παίξε το παιχνίδι.

Point. Δείξε.

Put a ✔ or a ✗. Βάλε ένα ✔ ή ένα ✗.

Read. Διάβασε.

Read and cross (X).

Διάβασε και βάλε (X).

Repeat. Επανέλαβε.

Say. Πες.

Sing along with the YAZOO Band.

Τραγούδησε μαζί με το συγκρότημα του YAZOO.

Stick. Κόλλησε.

Use. Χρησιμοποίησε.

What about you? Write.

Τι ισχύει για σένα; Γράψε.

Write. Γράψε.

Welcome to our zoo!
Καλώς ήρθατε στο ζωολογικό μας κήπο!

WL.01 **My name's ...**
To όνομά μου είναι ...

WL.02 **How are you?**
Τι κάνεις; Πώς είσαι;

WL.03 **I'm ...** (Εγώ) είμαι ...

WL.04 **an** ένας, μία, ένα

WL.05 **elephant** ελέφαντας

WL.06 **in** μέσα σε

WL.07 **the** ο, η, το

WL.08 **zoo** ζωολογικός κήπος

WL.09 **a** ένας, μία, ένα

WL.10 **monkey** μαϊμού

WL.11 **kangaroo** κανγκουρό

WL.12 **penguin** πιγκουίνος

WL.13 **tiger** τίγρης

WL.14 **keeper** φύλακας
(ζωολογικού κήπου)

WL.15 **I'm fine** (Εγώ) είμαι καλά

WL.16 **thank you** ευχαριστώ

WL.17 **We** Εμείς

WL.18 **love** αγαπώ

WL.19 **Hello!** Γεια!

WL.20 **Hi** Γεια

WL.21 **What's your name?**
Πώς σε λένε;

WL.22 **Goodbye.** Αντίο.

 1 Match.

1 What's your name?
2 How are you?
3 Hello!
4 I'm
5 Goodbye.

a Hi!
b an elephant.
c Goodbye.
d I'm fine, thank you!
e My name's Karla.

2 Put a ✔ or a ✗.

1 I'm Chatter. ✗

2 I'm Karla. ....

3 I'm Tag. ....

4 I'm Sally. ....

5 I'm Patty. ....

The alphabet
Το αλφάβητο

A.01 **Let's learn** Ας μάθουμε

A.02 **apple** μήλο

A.03 **bear** αρκούδα

A.04 **cat** γάτα

A.05 **dog** σκύλος

A.06 **flower** λουλούδι

A.07 **goat** κατσίκα

A.08 **hippo** ιπποπόταμος

A.09 **insect** έντομο

A.10 **jelly** ζελέ

A.11 **lion** λιοντάρι

A.12 **nest** φωλιά

A.13 **octopus** χταπόδι

A.14 **queen** βασίλισσα

A.15 **rabbit** κουνέλι

A.16 **snake** φίδι

A.17 **umbrella** ομπρέλα

A.18 **vulture** γύπας

A.19 **whale** φάλαινα

A.20 **fox** αλεπού

A.21 **yo-yo** γιογιό

A.22 **zebra** ζέβρα

1 **Choose and write.**

c a b o d e k f w g

1 ..a..pple

2 ....oat

3 ....og

4 ....angaroo

5 ....lower

6 ....at

7 ....lephant

8 ....ctopus

9 ....ear

10 ....hale

2 **Match.**

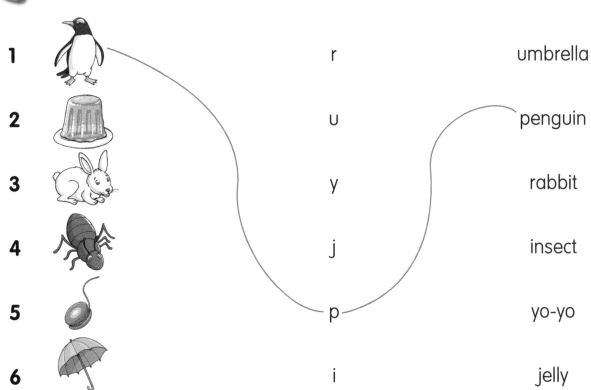

1   r   umbrella

2   u   penguin

3   y   rabbit

4   j   insect

5   p   yo-yo

6   i   jelly

3 **Circle.**

1	(hippo)	insect	jelly
2	octopus	lion	nest
3	penguin	fox	monkey
4	snake	queen	rabbit
5	dog	zebra	cat

Colours
Χρώματα

black
red  brown
blue

grey
 green
orange

purple
green
pink
yellow white

C.01 colours χρώματα	C.09 orange πορτοκαλί
 colour χρώμα	C.10 pink ροζ
C.02 red κόκκινο	C.11 brown καφέ
C.03 blue μπλε	C.12 white άσπρο
C.04 green πράσινο	C.13 and και
C.05 black μαύρο	C.14 too επίσης
C.06 yellow κίτρινο	C.15 for για
C.07 grey γκρι	C.16 you εσένα
C.08 purple μωβ	

1 Colour.

blue

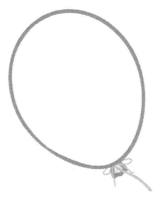

red

green

yellow

pink

purple

Numbers 1–10
Αριθμοί 1–10

N.01 **numbers** αριθμοί

 number αριθμός

N.02 **one** ένα

N.03 **two** δύο

N.04 **three** τρία

N.05 **four** τέσσερα

N.06 **five** πέντε

N.07 **six** έξι

N.08 **seven** επτά

N.09 **eight** οχτώ

N.10 **nine** εννέα

N.11 **ten** δέκα

1 Count and write.

1 ....two........

2 ....

3 ....

4 ....

5 ....

2 Match.

1 seven

2 nine

3 ten

4 eight

5 six

a

b

c

d

e

1 It's a school!
Είναι ένα σχολείο!

1.01   **school** σχολείο
1.02   **bag** τσάντα
1.03   **pencil** μολύβι
1.04   **pen** στυλό
1.05   **rubber** σβήστρα

1.06   **book** βιβλίο
1.07   **What's this?** Τί είναι αυτό;
1.08   **It's ...** Αυτό είναι ...
1.09   **my** (δικό) μου

What's this? Τι είναι αυτό;
It's a pencil. Είναι ένα μολύβι.
What's this? Τι είναι αυτό;
It's an umbrella. Είναι μία ομπρέλα.

Όταν θέλουμε να μάθουμε τι είναι κάτι, χρησιμοποιούμε τη φράση **What's this?** (Τι είναι αυτό;). Απαντάμε με τη φράση **It's** (Αυτός, -ή, -ό είναι) και βάζουμε **a** (ένας, μία, ένα) αν η επόμενη λέξη αρχίζει από σύμφωνο (**b, c, d, f, g, h, j, k, l, m, n, p, q, r, s, t, v, w, x, y, z**) και **an** (ένας, μία, ένα) αν η λέξη αρχίζει από φωνήεν (**a, e, i, o, u**).

1   Write.

1 ....bag....

2 ....

3 ....

4 ....

5 ....

6 ....

2   Write a or an.

1 What's this? It's ...a... school.
2 What's this? It's .... elephant.
3 What's this? It's .... tiger.

4 What's this? It's .... apple.
5 What's this? It's .... rubber.
6 What's this? It's .... insect.

2 Spell octopus.
Συλλάβισε τη λέξη χταπόδι.

2.01 **spell** συλλαβίζω

Spell Συλλάβισε/Συλλαβίστε

2.02 **chair** καρέκλα

2.03 **write** γράφω

write γράψε/γράψτε

2.04 **board** πίνακας

2.05 **be quiet** κάνε/κάντε ησυχία

2.06 **Yes.** Ναι.

2.07 **please** παρακαλώ

2.08 **Very good** Πολύ καλά

2.09 **on** πάνω σε

2.10 **is** είναι

2.11 **No.** Όχι.

It's a chair. The chair is brown.

Αυτή είναι μία καρέκλα. Η καρέκλα είναι καφέ.

It's an elephant. The elephant is white.

Αυτός είναι ένας ελέφαντας. Ο ελέφαντας είναι άσπρος.

Χρησιμοποιούμε το **a** και το **an** όταν μιλάμε για ένα οποιοδήποτε πρόσωπο, ζώο ή πράγμα. Όταν γνωρίζουμε για ποιο ακριβώς πράγμα μιλάμε ή πριν λίγο μιλήσαμε για αυτό, χρησιμοποιούμε το **the** αντί για τα **a** και **an**.

---

1 Find and write.

1 teirw ....write.........
2 lepsl ....
3 acihr ....

4 daorb ....
5 eb tueqi ....

2 Circle.

1 It's a / (an) apple. The apple is red.
2 It's a bag. The / A bag is yellow.
3 It's a / the rubber. The rubber is red and white.

4 It's a whale. A / The whale is blue.
5 It's a / an pen. The pen is black.

3 Cars and balls!
Αυτοκίνητα και μπάλες!

3.01 **car** αυτοκίνητο
 cars αυτοκίνητα
3.02 **ball** μπάλα
 balls μπάλες
3.03 **doll** κούκλα
 dolls κούκλες
3.04 **stickers** αυτοκόλλητα
 sticker αυτοκόλλητο
3.05 **crayon** κερομπογιά
 crayons κερομπογιές

3.06 **card** κάρτα
3.07 **What are they?** Τι είναι αυτοί, -ές, -ά;
3.08 **They're ...** Αυτοί, -ές, -ά είναι ...
3.09 **Come here** Έλα/Ελάτε εδώ
3.10 **me** μένα
3.11 **Lots of** Πολλοί, -ές, -ά
3.12 **big** μεγάλος, -η, -ο

a doll
μία κούκλα

two dolls
δύο κούκλες

What are they? Τί είναι αυτά;
They're pencils. Αυτά είναι μολύβια.

Βάζουμε **-s** στο τέλος μιας λέξης για να μιλήσουμε για περισσότερα από ένα πρόσωπα, ζώα ή πράγματα. Χρησιμοποιούμε τη φράση **What are they?** (Τι είναι αυτοί, -ές, -ά;) για να ρωτήσουμε για πολλά πρόσωπα, ζώα ή πράγματα.
Απαντάμε με τη φράση **They're** (Αυτοί, -ές, -ά είναι) και βάζουμε πάντα **-s** στο τέλος της λέξης για την οποία μιλάμε.

 1 **Do the crossword.**

1    **2**

3   **4**

5

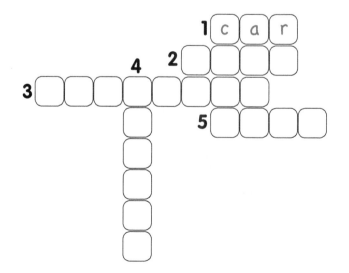

4 That's a robot!
Εκείνο είναι ένα ρομπότ!

4.01 **robot** ρομπότ

4.02 **birthday** γενέθλια

4.03 **cake** τούρτα

4.04 **present** δώρο

4.05 **watch** ρολόι (χεριού)

4.06 **This is ...** Αυτός, -ή, -ό είναι ...

4.07 **Happy Birthday** Χρόνια Πολλά, Ευτυχισμένα Γενέθλια

4.08 **your** (δικό) σου

4.09 **That is** Εκείνος, -η, -ο είναι

That's Εκείνος, -η, -ο είναι (σύντομος τύπος)

4.10 **lovely** υπέροχος, -η, -ο, θαυμάσιος, -α, -ο

4.11 **Guess!** Μάντεψε!/Μαντέψτε!

This is a present. Αυτό είναι ένα δώρο.

That is an elephant. Εκείνος είναι ένας ελέφαντας.

Για να μιλήσουμε και να δείξουμε ένα πρόσωπο, ζώο ή πράγμα που βρίσκεται κοντά μας, χρησιμοποιούμε τη φράση **This is** (Αυτός, -ή, -ό είναι), ενώ αν είναι μακριά μας χρησιμοποιούμε τη φράση **That is** (Εκείνος, -η, -ο είναι).

 1 **Find and circle. Then write.**

1	cake	q	p	r	e	s	e	n	t
2		x	f	o	t	d	r	m	o
3		y	l	b	k	c	a	k	e
4		i	s	o	w	n	c	z	v
5		a	w	t	a	j	u	g	k
		b	i	r	t	h	d	a	y
		f	o	e	c	l	r	p	b
		s	h	p	h	t	n	e	x

 2 **Write This is or That is.**

 1 That is a flower.

 2 .... a robot.

3 .... a penguin.

  4 .... an octopus.

Tag's chart

A/An

a flower

a**n** insect

a present

a**n** apple

What's this?

It's a book!

Plurals

one frog

four frog**s**

one cake

four cake**s**

They're presents.

Sally's Story
The frogs!
Οι βάτραχοι!

SS.01 **frog** βάτραχος
SS.02 **teacher** δάσκαλος, δασκάλα
SS.03 **close** κλείνω
    Close Κλείσε/Κλείστε
SS.04 **door** πόρτα
SS.05 **window** παράθυρο
SS.06 **stand up** σηκώνομαι
    Stand up Σήκω/Σηκωθείτε πάνω!
SS.07 **open** ανοίγω
    Open Άνοιξε/Ανοίξτε
SS.08 **sit down** κάθομαι κάτω
    Sit down Κάτσε/Καθίστε κάτω
SS.09 **What's that?** Τί είναι εκείνο;

Sally says ...

Για να δώσουμε μία οδηγία ή εντολή σ'ένα ή περισσότερα άτομα, λέμε κατευθείαν τη λέξη που θέλουμε να γίνει. Αν, όμως, μιλάμε σε μεγαλύτερους ανθρώπους ή θέλουμε να ζητήσουμε κάτι ευγενικά, βάζουμε τη λέξη **please** (παρακαλώ) στο τέλος της πρότασης.

Open the door!
Άνοιξε/Ανοίξτε την πόρτα!
Open the door, please.
Άνοιξε/Ανοίξτε την πόρτα, παρακαλώ!

1 Match.

1 Open
2 Stand
3 Sit
4 What's
5 Goodbye,

a down!
b that?
c frogs!
d the window!
e up!

2 Complete.

1 te a c h e r

2 c........s......

3 ......o....r

4 ....p..........

5  ......r....g

The Review 1

1 Circle.

1 book

2 chair

3 car

4 robot

5 teacher

2 Write.

1 ....watch....... **2** .... **3** ....

4 .... **5** .... **6** ....

3 **Draw and write.**

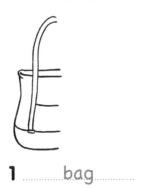

1 .... bag ....

2 ....

3 ....

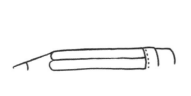

4 ....

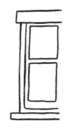

5 ....

4 **Match.**

1 It's a cake.

2 Sit down!

3 Stand up!

4 It's a pen.

5 They're three frogs.

6 Be quiet!

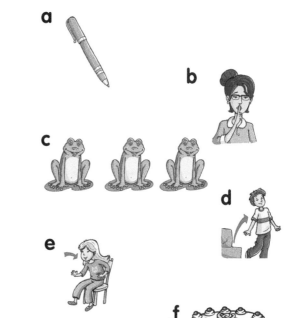

a

b

c

d

e

f

5 **Circle.**

1 It's .... window.
  a an   **(b)** a

2 What are they?
  a It's a sticker.   **b** They're stickers.

3 This is a car. .... car is red.
  a The   **b** A

4 What's this?
  a They're crayons. **b** It's a doll.

5 What are they?
  a They're three balls.
  b They're three ball.

5 She's pretty.
Αυτή είναι όμορφη.

5.01 **sunny** λιακάδα/ ηλιόλουστος καιρός

5.02 **family** οικογένεια

5.03 **mum** μαμά (σύντομη λέξη)

mother μητέρα

5.04 **dad** μπαμπάς (σύντομη λέξη)

father πατέρας

5.05 **brother** αδελφός

5.06 **sister** αδελφή

5.07 **It's sunny.** Έχει λιακάδα.

5.08 **He's** Αυτός είναι

5.09 **She's** Αυτή είναι

5.10 **pretty** όμορφος, -η, -ο

5.11 **Help!** Βοήθεια!

5.12 **Sorry** Συγγνώμη

5.13 **Clap** Χειροκρότησε/ Χειροκροτήστε

clap χειροκροτώ

5.14 **dance** χόρεψε/χορέψτε

dance χορεύω

5.15 **with** με

5.16 **about** για

I am Chatter. → I'm Chatter. Εγώ είμαι ο Τσάτερ.
You are Patty. → You're Patty. Εσύ είσαι η Πάτι.
He is Tag. → He's Tag. Αυτός είναι ο Ταγκ.
She is Sally. → She's Sally. Αυτή είναι η Σάλι.
It is a book. → It's a book. Αυτό είναι ένα βιβλίο.

> Όταν μιλάμε για αγόρι ή άνδρα χρησιμοποιούμε τη λέξη **he**, όταν μιλάμε για κορίτσι ή γυναίκα τη λέξη **she**, ενώ, όταν μιλάμε για ένα πράγμα ή ζώο, χρησιμοποιούμε το **it**.

1 Complete.

1 m..u.m

2 s.......s

3 b.......t

4 ....a

2 Write am, are or is.

1 He ...is... Chatter.

2 You .... Sally.

3 I .... Tag.

4 She .... Patty.

5 You .... my sister.

6 It .... a bag.

6 Is he your grandpa?
Είναι (αυτός) ο παππούς σου;

6.01 **grandpa** παππούς (σύντομη λέξη)
 grandfather παππούς
6.02 **baby** μωρό
6.03 **boy** αγόρι
6.04 **girl** κορίτσι
6.05 **grandma** γιαγιά (σύντομη λέξη)
 grandmother γιαγιά
6.06 **friend** φίλος, φίλη

6.07 **Are you …?** Είσαι εσύ …;
6.08 **No, I'm not.** Όχι, εγώ δεν είμαι.
6.09 **Is she …?** Είναι (αυτή) …;
6.10 **Yes, she is.** Ναι, (αυτή) είναι.
6.11 **Is he …?** Είναι (αυτός) …;
6.12 **No, he isn't.** Όχι, (αυτός) δεν είναι.

Am I a penguin? Yes, you are./No, you aren't.
Είμαι (εγώ) ένας πιγκουίνος;
Ναι, (εσύ) είσαι./Όχι, (εσύ) δεν είσαι.
Are you Chatter? Yes, I am./No, I'm not.
Είσαι (εσύ) ο Τσάτερ; Ναι, (εγώ) είμαι./Όχι, (εγώ) δεν είμαι.
Is he a friend? Yes, he is./No, he isn't.
Είναι (αυτός) ένας φίλος;
Ναι, (αυτός) είναι./Όχι, (αυτός) δεν είναι.
Is she a teacher? Yes, she is./No, she isn't.
Είναι (αυτή) μία δασκάλα;
Ναι, (αυτή) είναι./Όχι, (αυτή)δεν είναι.
Is it a baby? Yes, it is./No, it isn't.
Είναι (αυτό) ένα μωρό;
Ναι, (αυτό) είναι./Όχι, (αυτό) δεν είναι.

Για να κάνουμε ερώτηση, βάζουμε τα **Am, Are, Is** στην αρχή της πρότασης. Για να απαντήσουμε σύντομα βάζουμε **Yes** (Ναι) ή **No** (Όχι) στην αρχή της πρότασης, μετά το πρόσωπο (**I, you, he**, κτλ) και μετά τα **am/'m not, are/aren't** ή **is/isn't**.

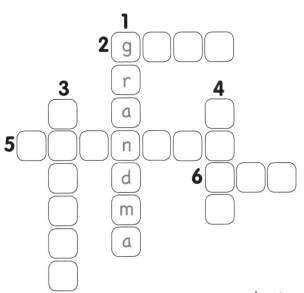

 1 **Do the crossword.**

1   2
3   4
5   6

Crossword:
2 g
1
r
3 a 4
5 n
d 6
m
a

7 We're cowboys.
Εμείς είμαστε καουμπόηδες.

7.01 **cowboy** καουμπόης

7.02 **box** κουτί

7.03 **clothes** ρούχα

7.04 **spy** κατάσκοπος

7.05 **dancer** χορευτής, χορεύτρια

7.06 **Wow!** Γουάου! (επιφώνημα έκπληξης και θαυμασμού)

7.07 **Let's go** Ας πάμε

7.08 **We're** Εμείς είμαστε

7.09 **Be careful** Πρόσεχε/Προσέχετε

7.10 **happy** χαρούμενος, -η, -ο

7.11 **today** σήμερα

7.12 **hands** χέρια

hand χέρι

We are friends. → We're friends.
Εμείς είμαστε φίλοι.
You are dancers. → You're dancers.
Εσείς είστε χορευτές.
They are kangaroos. → They're kangaroos.
Αυτά είναι κανγκουρό.

we εμείς
you εσύ κι εσείς
(ίδια λέξη!)
they αυτοί, αυτές, αυτά
(ίδια λέξη κι εδώ!)
Στα Ελληνικά μπορούμε να πούμε: Είμαστε φίλοι.
ή Εμείς είμαστε φίλοι.
Στα Αγγλικά, όμως, χρειαζόμαστε οπωσδήποτε το πρόσωπο:
We are friends.

 1 Write.

1 ....clothes....... **2** ....

3 .... **4** .... **5** ....

Are we pirates?
Είμαστε (εμείς) πειρατές;

8

8.01 **pirate** πειρατής

8.02 **clown** κλόουν

8.03 **king** βασιλιάς

8.04 **crown** στέμμα

8.05 **Are we ...?** Είμαστε (εμείς) ...;

8.06 **golden** χρυσαφένιος, -α, -ο

 gold χρυσός

8.07 **see** δες/δείτε

 see βλέπω

8.08 **What are we?** Τι είμαστε;

8.09 **Are they ...?**
Είναι (αυτοί, -ές, -ά) ...;

Are we teachers? Yes, you are./No, you aren't.
Είμαστε (εμείς) δασκάλες;
Ναι, (εσείς) είστε./Όχι, (εσείς) δεν είστε.
Are you friends? Yes, we are./No, we aren't.
Είστε (εσείς) φίλοι;
Ναι, (εμείς) είμαστε./Όχι, (εμείς) δεν είμαστε.
Are they monkeys? Yes, they are./No, they aren't.
Είναι (αυτές) μαϊμούδες;
Ναι, (αυτές) είναι./Όχι, (αυτές) δεν είναι.

Για να κάνουμε ερώτηση βάζουμε τις λέξεις ανάποδα.
We are friends.
Are we friends?
Για να απαντήσουμε σύντομα βάζουμε **Yes/No** στην αρχή της πρότασης, μετά το πρόσωπο (**we, you, they**) και μετά το **are/aren't**.

---

1 Match and write.

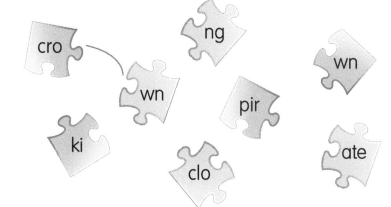

1 ...crown...

2 ....

3 ....

4 ....

2 Write.

1 Are you clowns?
Yes, ...we are...... .

2 Are they pirates?
No, ...

3 Are we queens?
Yes, ...

4 Are you elephants?
No, ...

5 Are we kings?
No, ...

6 Are they happy?
Yes, ...

Tag's chart

To be

I am Chatter. → I'm Chatter.
You are Patty. → You're Patty.
He is Tag. → He's Tag.
She is Sally. → She's Sally.
It is a book. → It's a book.
We are friends. → We're friends.
You are dancers. → You're dancers.
They are kangaroos. → They're kangaroos.

Am I a penguin?	Yes, you are./No, you aren't.
Are you Chatter?	Yes, I am./No, I'm not.
Is he a friend?	Yes, he is./No, he isn't.
Is she a teacher?	Yes, she is./No, she isn't.
Is it a monkey?	Yes, it is./No, it isn't.
Are we clowns?	Yes, you are./No, you aren't.
Are you pirates?	Yes, we are./No, we aren't.
Are they queens?	Yes, they are./No, they aren't.

I'm Tag. I'm a tiger, I'm not a lion.

Sally's Story
The grey duck
Η γκρι πάπια

SS.01 **duck** πάπια
SS.02 **happy** χαρούμενος, -η, -ο, ευτυχισμένος, -η, -ο
SS.03 **small** μικρός, -ή, -ό
SS.04 **big** μεγάλος, -η, -ο
SS.05 **sad** λυπημένος, -η, -ο
SS.06 **swan** κύκνος
SS.07 **Bye, bye** Γεια! (όταν φεύγουμε)
SS.08 **I love you** Σ'αγαπώ/Σας αγαπώ

Sally says ...

Για να περιγράψουμε κάτι ή κάποιον βάζουμε πρώτη τη λέξη που το περιγράφει.

It's a big bag.
Είναι μία μεγάλη τσάντα.
It's a happy duck.
Είναι μία ευτυχισμένη πάπια.

 1 Circle and write.

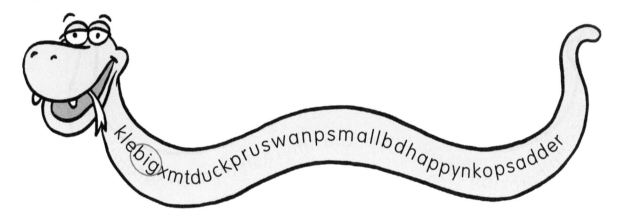

klebigxmtduckpruswanpsmallbdhappynkopsadder

1 ....big........   3 ....   5 ....

2 ....   4 ....   6 ....

 2 Find the odd one out.

1 big   (yellow)   small
2 yellow   grey   five
3 three   duck   swan

4 one   four   happy
5 happy   sad   big

The Review 2

1 Write.

1 ....box........ **2** .... **3** ....

4 .... **5** ....

2 Circle and write.

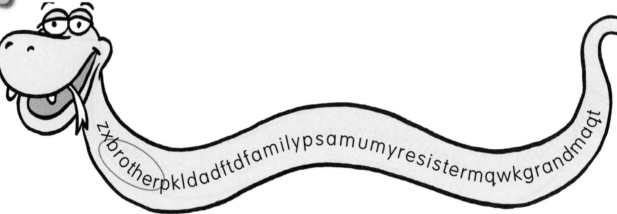

zxbrotherpkldadftdfamilypsamumyresistermqwkgrandmaqt

1 .....brother..... **3** .... **5** ....

2 .... **4** .... **6** ....

3 Put a ✔ or a ✗.

1 He's a clown. ✔ **2** She's happy. .... **3** They're five elephants. ....

4 We're pirates. .... **5** You're cowboys. .... **6** It's a duck. ....

4 Match.

1 They're a family.

2 We're friends.

3 She's a grandma.

4 You're big.

5 He's a boy.

6 I'm small.

a

b

c

d

e

f

 5 Circle.

1 Are they sad?
  a No, they aren't.   **b** They're friends.   **c** Yes, she is.

2 Is he a spy?
  a Yes, we are.   **b** Yes, he is.   **c** No, she isn't.

3 Are you a king?
  a No, we aren't.   **b** No, he isn't.   **c** No, I'm not.

4 Is it sunny?
  a Yes, it is.   **b** Yes, they are.   **c** No, you aren't.

5 Am I a baby?
  a Yes, it is.   **b** No, you aren't.   **c** Yes, we are.

6 Are you happy?
  a No, she isn't.   **b** Yes, they are.   **c** Yes, we are.

1 **Colour. Then choose and write.**

~~monkey~~   kangaroo   tiger   penguin

elephant   bear   lion   zebra

monkey

2 **Join and write.**

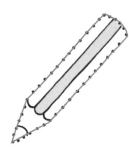      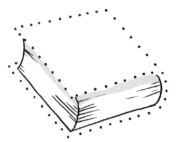

1 It's a pencil.   **2** ....   **3** ....

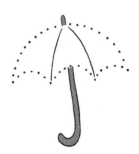   

4 ....   **5** ....

3 Read and draw.

1 two brown cakes

2 four red flowers

3 one blue window

4 three purple presents

5 five green apples

4 Match.

1 It's a car.

2 This is a clown.

3 He's a king.

4 They're pirates.

5 She's a teacher.

6 We're friends.

a

b

c

d

e

f

9

It's his kite.
Είναι ο χαρταετός του.

9.01 **kite** χαρταετός

9.02 **cloudy** συννεφιασμένος, -ή, -ό

It's cloudy. Έχει συννεφιά.

9.03 **computer game** παιχνίδι στον υπολογιστή

9.04 **old** παλιός, -ά, -ό

9.05 **radio** ραδιόφωνο

9.06 **new** καινούριος, -α, -ο

9.07 **bike** ποδήλατο

bicycle ποδήλατο

9.08 **his** (δικό) του (για αγόρι ή άνδρα)

9.09 **What a mess!** Τι ακαταστασία!

9.10 **her** (δικό) της

9.11 **Come back** Έλα/Ελάτε πίσω

9.12 **Its** (δικό) του (για ζώο ή πράγμα)

9.13 **terrible** τρομερός, -ή, -ό

---

my (δικό) μου	**her** (δικό) της
your (δικό) σου	**its** (δικό) του
his (δικό) του	

It's my bike. (Αυτό) είναι το ποδήλατό μου.

They're your books. (Αυτά) είναι τα βιβλία σου.

This is his ball. Αυτή είναι η μπάλα του.

That is her present. Εκείνο είναι το δώρο της.

This is an apple. Its colour is green.
Αυτό είναι ένα μήλο. Το χρώμα του είναι πράσινο.

> Όταν θέλουμε να δείξουμε σε ποιον ανήκει κάτι, χρησιμοποιούμε τις λέξεις **my**, **your**, **his**, **her**, **its**. Αυτές τις λέξεις τις βάζουμε πάντα πριν από το ουσιαστικό για το οποίο θέλουμε να μιλήσουμε.

---

1) Match.

1	sunny	**a**	stand up
2	new	**b**	sad
3	open	**c**	cloudy
4	sit down	**d**	old
5	happy	**e**	close
6	big	**f**	small

2) Circle.

1 She's a girl and her / your name is Helen.

2 He's a teacher and this is his / her book.

3 You're Anna and this is his / your kite.

4 I'm Emma and this is my / its sister.

10 They're our toys.
Είναι τα παιχνίδια μας.

10.01 **toys** παιχνίδια
 toy παιχνίδι
10.02 **rollerblades** πατίνια
 rollerblade πατίνι
10.03 **train** τρένο
10.04 **slow** αργός, -ή, -ό
10.05 **fast** γρήγορος, -η, -ο
10.06 **winner** νικητής, νικήτρια

10.07 **prize** βραβείο
10.08 **our** (δικό) μας
10.09 **Here (is, are)** Να, Ορίστε
 here εδώ
10.10 **their** (δικό) τους
10.11 **Let's race!** Ας παραβγούμε!
10.12 **favourite** αγαπημένος, -η, -ο

Για να πούμε ότι κάτι ανήκει σε εμάς, σε εσάς ή σε αυτούς, χρησιμοποιούμε τις λέξεις **our, your, their**.

our (δικό/δικά) μας
your (δικό/δικά) σας
their (δικό/δικά) τους
This is **our** family. Αυτή είναι η οικογένειά μας.
It's **your** present. Αυτό είναι το δώρο σας.
They're winners. This is **their** prize. Είναι νικητές. Αυτό είναι το βραβείο τους.

1 **Do the crossword. Then find the secret word.**

 1
 2
 3
 4
5

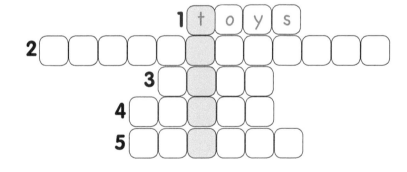

2 **Choose and write.**

~~my~~   your   their   our

1 I'm Tag. They're ___my___ toys.
2 Look at Karla and Patty. That's _____ doll.

3 Look at my family. This is _____ new house.
4 Hi, boys! Is this _____ teacher?

11 I've got a pet.
Έχω ένα κατοικίδιο (ζώο).

11.01 **leg** πόδι (πάνω από τον αστράγαλο)

11.02 **body** σώμα

11.03 **head** κεφάλι

11.04 **wing** φτερό

11.05 **hand** χέρι (κάτω από τον καρπό)

11.06 **arm** χέρι (πάνω από τον καρπό)

11.07 **feet** πόδια

foot πόδι (κάτω από τον αστράγαλο)

11.08 **I've got** Έχω

11.09 **pet** κατοικίδιο (ζώο)

11.10 **It's got** (Αυτό) έχει

11.11 **beautiful** όμορφος, -η, -ο

11.12 **She's got** (Αυτή) έχει

11.13 **lucky** τυχερός, -ή, -ό

11.14 **They've got** (Αυτοί, -ές, -ά) έχουν

11.15 **Oh, dear!** Ω, Θεέ μου!

11.16 **We've got** Έχουμε

11.17 **all** όλοι, -ες, -α

11.18 **now** τώρα

11.19 **to the beat** στο ρυθμό

11.20 **turn around** κάνε/κάντε μία στροφή

11.21 **Stamp** Χτύπησε/Χτυπήστε (τα πόδια)

stamp χτυπώ τα πόδια

11.22 **touch** άγγιξε/αγγίξτε

touch αγγίζω

11.23 **ground** έδαφος

11.24 **then** μετά

I have ('ve) got a bike. Έχω ένα ποδήλατο.
You have ('ve) got two books. Έχεις δύο βιβλία.
He/She/It has ('s) got a kite. (Αυτός, -ή, -ό) έχει ένα χαρταετό.
We have ('ve) got rollerblades. Έχουμε πατίνια.
You have ('ve) got a sister. Έχετε μία αδερφή.
They have ('ve) got lots of friends.
(Αυτοί, -ές, -ά) έχουν πολλούς φίλους.

Όταν θέλουμε να περιγράψουμε τι έχουμε, χρησιμοποιούμε τις φράσεις **have got** και **has got**. Have got βάζουμε μετά από τα πρόσωπα **I**, **you**, **we**, **they** και **has got** μετά από τα **he**, **she**, **it**.

 1 **Write.**

1 .... head ....

2 ....

3 ....

4 ....

5 ....

6 ....

12 Have we got all the insects?
Έχουμε όλα τα έντομα;

12.01 **ear** αυτί

12.02 **mouth** στόμα

12.03 **nose** μύτη

12.04 **eye** μάτι

12.05 **butterfly** πεταλούδα

12.06 **hair** μαλλιά

12.07 **hair slide** κοκκαλάκι μαλλιών

12.08 **everywhere** παντού

12.09 **Quick!** Γρήγορα!

12.10 **Atishoo!** Αψού
(επιφώνημα φτερνίσματος)

12.11 **Have we got ...?** Έχουμε ...;

12.12 **No, we haven't.** Όχι, δεν έχουμε.

12.13 **Has it got ...?** Έχει (αυτό);

12.14 **Yes, it has.** Ναι, (αυτό) έχει.

12.15 **No, I haven't.** Όχι, δεν έχω.

Has she got a doll? Yes, she has./No, she hasn't.
Έχει (αυτή) μία κούκλα; Ναι, έχει./Όχι, δεν έχει.
Have they got a car?
Yes, they have./No, they haven't.
Έχουν (αυτοί, -ές, -ά) ένα αυτοκίνητο;
Ναι, έχουν. Όχι, δεν έχουν.

Όταν θέλουμε να ρωτήσουμε αν κάποιος έχει κάτι, βάζουμε τα **Have/Has** στην αρχή της πρότασης. Για να απαντήσουμε σύντομα, βάζουμε **Yes/No** στην αρχή της πρότασης, μετά το πρόσωπο (**I, you, he**, κτλ) και μετά τα **have/haven't, has/hasn't**. Δεν επαναλαμβάνουμε τη λέξη **got**.

 1 Choose and write.

eye   nose   mouth   ear   ~~hair~~

1 ....hair..........

2 ....

3 ....

4 ....

5 ....

Tag's chart

Have got

I have got a bike. → I've got a bike.
You have got a train. → You've got a train.
He has got a kite. → He's got a kite.
She has got a doll. → She's got a doll.
It has got two ears. → It's got two ears.
We have got a radio. → We've got a radio.
You have got a computer game. → You've got a computer game.
They have got rollerblades. → They've got rollerblades.

Have I got a bike?   Yes, you have./No, you haven't.
Have you got a train?   Yes, I have./No, I haven't.
Has he got a kite?   Yes, he has./No, he hasn't.
Has she got a doll?   Yes, she has./No, she hasn't.
Has it got two ears?   Yes, it has./No, it hasn't.
Have we got a radio?   Yes, you have./No, you haven't.
Have you got a computer game?   Yes, we have./No, we haven't.
Have they got rollerblades?   Yes, they have./No, they haven't.

I've got a watch!

Sally's Story
Circus boy!
Το παιδί του τσίρκου!

SS.01 **circus** τσίρκο
SS.02 **funny** αστείος, -α, -ο
SS.03 **long** μακρύς, -ιά, -ύ
SS.04 **short** κοντός, -ή, -ό
SS.05 **strong** δυνατός, -ή, -ό
SS.06 **trunk** προβοσκίδα
SS.07 **star** αστέρι, σταρ
SS.08 **very** πολύ
SS.09 **Hooray!** Ζήτω!

Sally says...

Η λέξη **small** σημαίνει μικρός, αλλά τη χρησιμοποιούμε για να μιλήσουμε κυρίως για μέγεθος. Έτσι **a small boy** είναι ένα μικρόσωμο αγόρι κι όχι ένα αγόρι μικρό σε ηλικία.

 1 **Write.**

1 ..... dancer ...... **2** .... **3** ....

4 .... **5** ....

 2 **Put a ✔ or a ✗. Then correct the wrong sentences.**

1 It's a watch. .... X .... It's a trunk. ....

2 She's got short hair. ....

3 He's funny. ....

4 It's small. ....

The Review 3

1 **Choose and write.**

leg   ear   ~~arm~~   mouth   nose   foot   eye

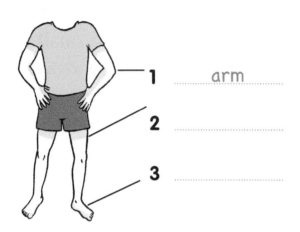

1 ....arm....
2 ....
3 ....

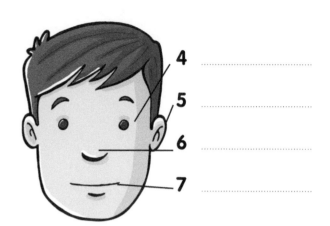

4 ....
5 ....
6 ....
7 ....

2 **Choose and write.**

short   sad   ~~new~~   small   fast

1 old   ....new....
2 slow   ....
3 long   ....

4 big   ....
5 happy   ....

3 **Find and write.**

1   eikb   ....bike....

2    itke   ....

3   fyutbterl   ....

4   ccrisu   ....

5   rllleeasbdro   ....

4 **Read and answer.**

1 Has Mandy got small eyes? .... Yes, she has. ....
2 Has Mandy got two legs? ....
3 Has Gerry got a small nose? ....
4 Has Gerry got a small mouth? ....
5 Have they got funny hair? ....
6 Have they got wings? ....

 5 **What about you? Circle.**

1 Have you got a sister?   Yes, I have. / No, I haven't.
2 Have you got a computer?   Yes, I have. / No, I haven't.
3 Have you got a pet?   Yes, I have. / No, I haven't.
4 Have you got a bike?   Yes, I have. / No, I haven't.
5 Have you got short hair?   Yes, I have. / No, I haven't.

13 There's a town.
Υπάρχει μία πόλη.

13.01 **house** σπίτι

13.02 **swimming pool** πισίνα

13.03 **park** πάρκο

13.04 **river** ποτάμι

13.05 **tree** δέντρο

13.06 **playground** παιδική χαρά

13.07 **children** παιδιά

child παιδί

13.08 **fantastic** φανταστικά

13.09 **here** εδώ

13.10 **There's** Υπάρχει

13.11 **town** πόλη

13.12 **There are** Υπάρχουν

13.13 **go** πηγαίνω

13.14 **animals** ζώα

animal ζώο

13.15 **cockatoos** παπαγάλοι

cockatoo παπαγάλος (μεγάλος με λοφίο)

There is a river in the park.
Υπάρχει ένα ποτάμι μέσα στο πάρκο.
There are children in the playground.
Υπάρχουν παιδιά στην παιδική χαρά.

Για να πούμε τι υπάρχει κάπου, χρησιμοποιούμε τη φράση **There is** (Υπάρχει), ενώ για να πούμε ότι υπάρχουν περισσότερα από ένα πράγματα χρησιμοποιούμε το **There are** (Υπάρχουν).

1 Put a ✔ or a ✗.

1 a playground ✔

2 a town ....

3 a park ....

4 a flower ....

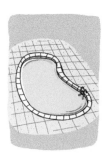

5 a swimming pool ....

14 Where's Chatter?
Πού είναι ο Chatter;

14.01 **hot** ζεστός, -ή, -ό

14.02 **treehouse** σπιτάκι πάνω σε δέντρο

14.03 **shop** κατάστημα, μαγαζί

14.04 **swing** κούνια

14.05 **slide** τσουλήθρα

14.06 **climbing frame** πλαίσιο σκαρφαλώματος, μονόζυγο

14.07 **bus** λεωφορείο

14.08 **Where's ...?** Πού είναι ... (αυτός, -ή, -ό);

14.09 **It's hot.** Έχει ζέστη.

14.10 **I don't know.** Δεν ξέρω.

14.11 **under** κάτω από

14.12 **next to** δίπλα σε

14.13 **Where are ...?** Πού είναι ...;

14.14 **There isn't** Δεν υπάρχει

Where is the bike?
Πού είναι το ποδήλατο;
Where are the trees?
Πού είναι τα δέντρα;
The pencil is in the bag.
Το μολύβι είναι μέσα στην τσάντα.
Patty is on the swing.
Η Πάτι είναι πάνω στην κούνια.
There are flowers under the slide.
Υπάρχουν λουλούδια κάτω από την τσουλήθρα.
Chatter is next to the bus.
Ο Τσάτερ είναι δίπλα στο λεωφορείο.

Όταν θέλουμε να ρωτήσουμε πού βρίσκεται ένα ή πού βρίσκονται πολλά πρόσωπα, ζώα ή πράγματα, λέμε **Where is** για ένα και **Where are** για πολλά.
Όταν θέλουμε να δείξουμε πού μπορούμε να βρούμε κάτι ή κάποιον, χρησιμοποιούμε το **in** (μέσα σε), **on** (πάνω σε), **under** (κάτω από) και **next to** (δίπλα σε).

 1 Circle.

1  It's a swimming pool / (climbing frame.)

2  This is a bus / car.

3  It's a shop / treehouse.

4  It's a swing / slide.

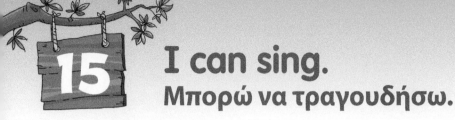

15   I can sing.
Μπορώ να τραγουδήσω.

15.01 **sing** τραγουδώ

15.02 **jump** πηδώ

15.03 **high** ψηλός, -ή, -ό

🐾   **high** ψηλά

15.04 **ride** καβαλώ

15.05 **swim** κολυμπώ

15.06 **climb** σκαρφαλώνω

15.07 **play the guitar** παίζω κιθάρα

15.08 **can** μπορώ

15.09 **that's terrible** είναι χάλια

15.10 **It's OK** Εντάξει, Δεν πειράζει

15.11 **sea** θάλασσα

15.12 **sky** ουρανός

I can swim.   Μπορώ να κολυμπήσω.

You can swim.   Μπορείς να κολυμπήσεις.

He can swim.   (Αυτός) μπορεί να κολυμπήσει.

She can swim.   (Αυτή) μπορεί να κολυμπήσει.

It can swim.   (Αυτό) μπορεί να κολυμπήσει.

We can swim.   Μπορούμε να κολυμπήσουμε.

You can swim.   Μπορείτε να κολυμπήσετε.

They can swim.   (Αυτοί, -ές, -ά) μπορούν να κολυμπήσουν.

Για να πούμε τι μπορούμε να κάνουμε, χρησιμοποιούμε το **can** (μπορώ) και τη λέξη που δείχνει τι μπορούμε να κάνουμε.

1   Match.

1   jump

2   ride

3   swim

4   climb

5   play the guitar

a

b

c

d

e

16 Can you skip?
Μπορείς να χοροπηδήσεις;

16.01 **skip** χοροπηδώ

16.02 **rollerblade** κάνω πατίνια

16.03 **fly** πετώ

16.04 **do a handstand** κάνω κατακόρυφο

16.05 **walk** περπατώ

16.06 **run** τρέχω

16.07 **carry** κουβαλώ

16.08 **Can you ...?** Μπορείς ...;

16.09 **I can't** Δε μπορώ

16.10 **things** πράγματα

thing πράγμα

16.11 **everyone** όλοι

16.12 **We can't** Δε μπορούμε

I/You/We/They can't play.

He/She/It can't play.

Can you run? Yes, I can./No, I can't.

Μπορείς να τρέξεις; Ναι, μπορώ./Όχι, δεν μπορώ.

Can she run? Yes, she can./No, she can't.

Μπορεί (αυτή) να τρέξει;
Ναι, μπορεί./Όχι, δε μπορεί.

Can they run? Yes, they can./No, they can't.

Μπορούν (αυτοί, -ές, -ά) να τρέξουν;
Ναι, μπορούν./Όχι, δε μπορούν.

Για να πούμε πως κάποιος δε μπορεί να κάνει κάτι, χρησιμοποιούμε το **can't**.
Όταν θέλουμε να ρωτήσουμε αν κάποιος μπορεί να κάνει κάτι, βάζουμε το **Can** στην αρχή τις πρότασης. Απαντάμε σύντομα με **Yes/No** στην αρχή της πρότασης, μετά το πρόσωπο (**I, you, he,** κτλ.) και μετά το **can/can't**.

---

1 **Write.**

1 ....fly..........

2 ....

3 ....

4 ....

5 ....

6 ....

Tag's chart

Can

I can sing.	I can't sing.
You can sing.	You can't sing.
He can sing.	He can't sing.
She can sing.	She can't sing.
It can sing.	It can't sing.
We can sing.	We can't sing.
You can sing.	You can't sing.
They can sing.	They can't sing.

Can I sing?	Yes, you can./No, you can't.
Can you sing?	Yes, I can./No, I can't.
Can he sing?	Yes, he can./No, he can't.
Can she sing?	Yes, she can./No, she can't.
Can it sing?	Yes, it can./No, it can't.
Can we sing?	Yes, you can./No, you can't.
Can you sing?	Yes, we can./No, we can't.
Can they sing?	Yes, they can./No, they can't.

I can't fly, but I can ride a bike!

Sally's Story
Where's my mobile phone?
Πού είναι το κινητό μου τηλέφωνο;

SS.01 **mobile phone** κινητό τηλέφωνο

SS.02 **desk** γραφείο, θρανίο

SS.03 **cupboard** ντουλάπι

SS.04 **computer** υπολογιστής

SS.05 **bookcase** βιβλιοθήκη (το έπιπλο)

SS.06 **table** τραπέζι

SS.07 **bed** κρεβάτι

SS.08 **living room** σαλόνι

SS.09 **What's the matter?** Τι συμβαίνει;

SS.10 **idea** ιδέα

SS.11 **What's your number?** Ποιο είναι το νούμερο του τηλεφώνου σου;

1 Do the crossword.

1

2

3

4

5

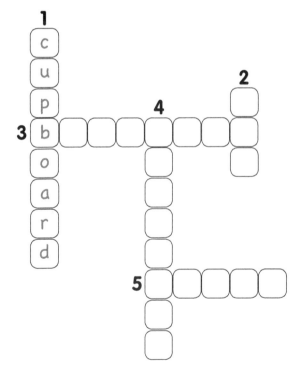

2 Find the odd one out.

1 desk table (cupboard)

2 bed swing slide

3 eye ear thing

4 computer book mobile phone

5 guitar bookcase book

1 **Choose and write.**

slide   bed   ~~swing~~   climbing frame   bookcase   cupboard

Playground	House
swing	

2 **Write yes or no.**

1 This is a mobile phone. _yes_

2 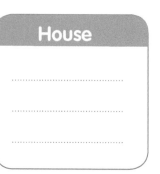 It's a town. ....

3 It's a computer. ....

4 This is a shop. ....

5 It's a park. ....

3 **Find and write.**

1 ...... tree ......
2 ....
3 ....
4 ....
5 ....
6 ....

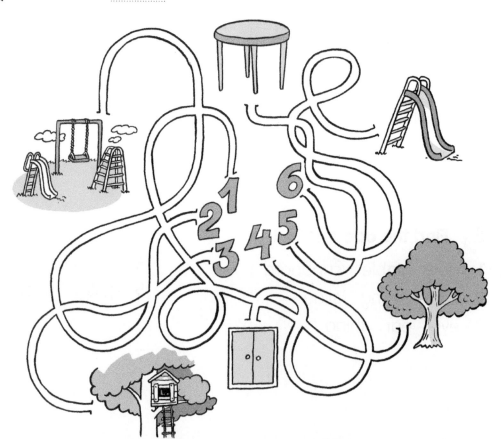

4 Read and answer.

1 Can an elephant fly?   No, _____it can't_____ .
2 Can whales swim?   Yes, _____ .
3 Can snakes do a handstand?   No, _____ .
4 Can monkeys climb on trees?   Yes, _____ .
5 Can you play the guitar?   _____

5 Look and write.

swim	✗	✔
jump	✔	✔
play the guitar	✗	✗
climb	✔	✗
run	✔	✔

1 Chatter _____can't_____ swim.
2 Patty _____jump.
3 Chatter and Patty _____ run.
4 Chatter and Patty _____ play the guitar.
5 Chatter _____ climb.

6 Write There is or There are.

1 Look! _____There are_____ stars in the sky.

2 Listen! _____ a mobile phone on the table.

3 Let's go. _____ lots of shops in the town.

4 Let's play. _____ a climbing frame in the playground.

5 What a mess! _____ clothes on the bed.

17 I'm playing a game!
Παίζω ένα παιχνίδι!

17.01 **play** παίζω

17.02 **do my homework** κάνω τις εργασίες του σχολείου στο σπίτι

17.03 **read** διαβάζω

17.04 **sleep** κοιμάμαι

17.05 **hide** κρύβω, κρύβομαι

17.06 **water pistol** νεροπίστολο

17.07 **come** έρχομαι

17.08 **away** μακριά

17.09 **from** από

I am singing. → I'm singing.
Τραγουδώ.
You are climbing. → You're climbing.
Σκαρφαλώνεις.
He is hiding. → He's hiding.
(Αυτός) κρύβεται.
She is walking. → She's walking.
(Αυτή) περπατάει.
It is jumping. → It's jumping.
(Αυτό) πηδάει.

Για να μιλήσουμε για κάτι που γίνεται τώρα, ή για κάτι που κάποιος κάνει αυτή τη στιγμή που μιλάμε, χρησιμοποιούμε το πρόσωπο, τα **am**, **are**, **is** και το ρήμα με την κατάληξη **-ing**. Δηλαδή: πρόσωπο + **am/are/is** + ρήμα + **-ing**
I am playing with my friends.
Παίζω με τους φίλους μου. (ΤΩΡΑ!)

 1 Choose and write.

read   do my homework   ~~play~~   sleep   hide   come

1  ....play............

2 ....

3 ....

4 ....

5 ....

6 ....

18 They're having a shower.
Κάνουν ντουζ.

18.01 **have a shower** κάνω ντουζ

18.02 **trousers** παντελόνι

18.03 **T-shirt** κοντομάνικο μπλουζάκι

18.04 **shoes** παπούτσια

    shoe παπούτσι

18.05 **skirt** φούστα

18.06 **dress** φόρεμα

18.07 **sweater** πουλόβερ

18.08 **wear** φορώ

We are dancing. → We're dancing.
Χορεύουμε.
You are sleeping. → You're sleeping.
Κοιμάστε.
They are reading. → They're reading.
(Αυτοί, -ές, -ά) διαβάζουν.

Στον πληθυντικό αριθμό χρησιμοποιούμε:
πρόσωπο + **are** + ρήμα + **-ing**.
We are reading a book.
Διαβάζουμε ένα βιβλίο. (ΤΩΡΑ!)

1 Read and draw.

1 trousers	**2** a skirt	**3** a T-shirt

4 shoes	**5** a sweater

2 Put a ✔ or a ✗. Then correct the wrong sentences.

1 We wearing sweaters.   _X_   We are wearing sweaters.

2 You are playing in the playground.

3 They jumping.

4 We are having a shower.

5 She is read.

19 They aren't swimming!
Δεν κολυμπούν!

19.01 **basketball** μπάσκετ

19.02 **volleyball** βόλεϊ

19.03 **football** ποδόσφαιρο

19.04 **tennis** τένις

19.05 **idea** ιδέα

19.06 **tired** κουρασμένος, -η, -ο

19.07 **splash** πλατσουρίζω

Αν θέλουμε να πούμε πως κάποιος δεν κάνει κάτι τώρα, βάζουμε τη λέξη **not** μετά τα **am**, **is**, **are**.
I'm not having a shower.
Δεν κάνω ντουζ.

I am not sleeping. → I'm not sleeping.
Δεν κοιμάμαι.

You are not sleeping. → You aren't sleeping.
Δεν κοιμάσαι.

He is not sleeping. → He isn't sleeping.
(Αυτός) δεν κοιμάται.

She is not sleeping. → She isn't sleeping.
(Αυτή) δεν κοιμάται.

It is not sleeping. → It isn't sleeping.   (Αυτό) δεν κοιμάται.

We are not sleeping. → We aren't sleeping.   Δεν κοιμόμαστε.

You are not sleeping. → You aren't sleeping.   Δεν κοιμάστε.

They are not sleeping. → They aren't sleeping.   (Αυτοί, -ές, -ά) δεν κοιμούνται.

1 Circle.

1 (He's sleeping.) /
He isn't sleeping.

2 We aren't having a shower. / We're having a shower.

3 She's wearing a skirt. / She isn't wearing a skirt.

4  She's playing volleyball. / She isn't playing volleyball.

5 He's playing tennis. / He isn't playing tennis.

20 Are they sleeping?
Κοιμούνται;

20.01 **dream** ονειρεύομαι

20.02 **noise** θόρυβος

20.03 **eat** τρώω

20.04 **drink** πίνω

20.05 **upstairs** το επάνω πάτωμα

20.06 **roar** βρυχώμαι

20.07 **snore** ροχαλίζω

20.08 **What are they doing?** Τι κάνουν;

20.09 **us** εμάς

20.10 **picture** εικόνα

Am I eating? | Yes, you are./No, you aren't.
Τρώω; | Ναι, (τρως)./Όχι, (δεν τρως).
Are you eating? | Yes, I am./No, I'm not.
Τρως; | Ναι, (τρώω)./Όχι, (δεν τρώω).
Is he eating? | Yes, he is./No, he isn't.
Τρώει (αυτός); | Ναι, (τρώει)./Όχι, (δεν τρώει).
Is she eating? | Yes, she is./No, she isn't.
Τρώει (αυτή); | Ναι, (τρώει)./Όχι, (δεν τρώει).
Is it eating? | Yes, it is./No, it isn't.
Τρώει (αυτό); | Ναι, (τρώει)./Όχι, (δεν τρώει).
Are we eating? | Yes, you are./No, you aren't.
Τρώμε; | Ναι, (τρώτε)./Όχι, (δεν τρώτε).
Are you eating? | Yes, we are./No, we aren't.
Τρώτε; | Ναι, (τρώμε)./Όχι, (δεν τρώμε).
Are they eating? | Yes, they are./No, they aren't.
Τρώνε (αυτοί, -ές, -ά); | Ναι, (τρώνε)./Όχι, (δεν τρώνε).

Όταν θέλουμε να ρωτήσουμε αν κάποιος κάνει κάτι τώρα, αλλάζουμε τη σειρά των λέξεων.
She is sleeping.
Is she sleeping?
Για να απαντήσουμε σύντομα βάζουμε το **Yes/No** στην αρχή της πρότασης, μετά το πρόσωπο (**I, you, he**, κτλ) και μετά τα **am/'m not**, **are/aren't** ή **is/isn't**. Δεν επαναλαμβάνουμε το ρήμα με την κατάληξη **-ing**.

 1 Match.

a

b

c

d

1 drink **2** dream **3** eat **4** noise

Tag's chart

Present continuous

I am singing. → I'm singing.
You are singing. → You're singing.
He is singing. → He's singing.
She is singing. → She's singing.
It is singing. → It's singing.
We are singing. → We're singing.
You are singing. → You're singing.
They are singing. → They're singing.

I am not singing. → I'm not singing.
You are not singing. → You aren't singing.
He is not singing. → He isn't singing.
She is not singing. → She isn't singing.
It is not singing. → It isn't singing.
We are not singing. → We aren't singing.
You are not singing.→ You aren't singing.
They are not singing. → They aren't singing.

Am I singing?	Yes, you are./No, you aren't.
Are you singing?	Yes, I am./No, I'm not.
Is he singing?	Yes, he is./No, he isn't.
Is she singing?	Yes, she is./No, she isn't.
Is it singing?	Yes, it is./No, it isn't.
Are we singing?	Yes, you are./No, you aren't.
Are you singing?	Yes, we are./No, we aren't.
Are they singing?	Yes, they are./No, they aren't.

I'm hiding under the bag!

Sally's Story
Jane and the giant
Η Τζέιν και ο γίγαντας

SS.01 **giant** γίγαντας

SS.02 **hear** ακούω

SS.03 **living room** σαλόνι

SS.04 **bathroom** μπάνιο

SS.05 **kitchen** κουζίνα

SS.06 **bedroom** υπνοδωμάτιο

SS.07 **ghost** φάντασμα

SS.08 **toast** φρυγανισμένο ψωμί

SS.09 **Goodnight** Καληνύχτα

SS.10 **says** (αυτός, -ή, -ό) λέει

SS.11 **Sweet dreams** Όνειρα γλυκά

Sally says ...

Όταν κάποιος πηγαίνει να κοιμηθεί και μας λέει 'καληνύχτα', μπορούμε να απαντήσουμε:

Sweet dreams. Όνειρα γλυκά.

1 **Choose and write.**

toys   bed   bookcase   ~~bedroom~~   bathroom

I love my (**1**) ....bedroom............ . It's got a (**2**)

.... and a (**3**) .... There are

lots of (**4**) .... and there is a (**5**)

.... in my bedroom too!

2 **Find the odd one out.**

1 eat   drink   (water pistol)

2 living room   bookcase   bedroom

3 toast   dream   snore

4 Goodnight.   Goodbye.
    Sweet dreams.

5 look   hear   listen

1 **Choose and write.**

basketball   trousers   ~~tennis~~   sweater   volleyball   dress

.... tennis ....

....

....

....

....

2 **Match.**

1 eat

2 drink

3 sleep

4 read

5 wear

6 have a shower

a

b

c

d

e

f

3 **Join the house words.**

bathroom	football	water pistol
giant	kitchen	hear
idea	ghost	bedroom
dream	living room	noise
tired	snore	shower

4 Put a ✔ or a ✗.

1 She isn't playing. ....✗...........

2 He's sleeping. ....

3 He's having a shower. ....

4 You're wearing sweaters. ....

5 It isn't roaring. ....

 5 Write.

1 Is Trumpet sleeping?   No, he ....isn't............. .
2 Are the cowboys dreaming?   No, they ....
3 Is Karla playing basketball? No, she ....
4 Are you wearing a green T-shirt? Yes, I ....
5 Is the dog roaring?   No, it ....
6 Are we doing our homework?   Yes, you ....

6 Circle.

1 Are you hiding in the treehouse?

   a No, I'm not.   **b** No, they aren't.   **c** Yes, she is.

2 Look! He's wearing blue shoes. He .... red shoes.

   a aren't wearing   **b** is   **c** isn't wearing

3 What are they doing?

   a She's reading a book.   **b** They're having a shower.   **c** They are giants.

4 Is Trumpet snoring?

   a No, he is.   **b** Yes, he is.   **c** Yes, he isn't.

5 The baby is sleeping.

   a Sweet dreams!   **b** Jump into bed!   **c** What a mess!

1 Draw a 🙂 or a 🙁 .

🙂 **There is**    🙁 **There isn't**

1 a swimming pool 🙁
2 a treehouse ....
3 a ball ....

4 a doll ....
5 a kite ....
6 a bike ....

2 **Match and colour.**

I they you he we it she

my your her our his its their

3 Match.

1 She's playing the guitar.

2 It's green and it has got four legs.

3 She's doing a handstand.

4 You can see clowns there.

5 Look! He's climbing.

6 Where's my mobile phone?

a

b

c

d

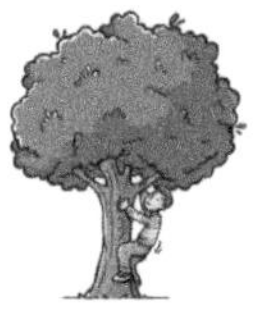

e

f

4 Read and draw.

1 There is a tree next to the river.

2 There are three butterflies in the sky.

3 There is a ball on the bed.

4 There are two presents under the table.

21 These are crabs.
Αυτά είναι καβούρια.

21.01 **crab** καβούρι
21.02 **raining** βρέχει
21.03 **fish** ψάρι
fish ψάρια
21.04 **dolphin** δελφίνι
21.05 **turtle** θαλάσσια χελώνα

21.06 **camera** φωτογραφική μηχανή
21.07 **take a photo** βγάζω φωτογραφία
21.08 **Yes, of course.** Ναι, βέβαια.
21.09 **What are these?** Τι είναι αυτά;
21.10 **These are** Αυτά είναι

This is a dolphin.
Αυτό είναι ένα δελφίνι.
These are dolphins.
Αυτά είναι δελφίνια.

Όταν θέλουμε να δείξουμε ένα πρόσωπο, ζώο ή πράγμα που βρίσκεται κοντά μας χρησιμοποιούμε τη φράση **This is** (Αυτό είναι).
Εάν, όμως, είναι περισσότερα από ένα και είναι κοντά μας, τότε λέμε **These are** (Αυτά είναι).

1 Do the crossword.

1
2
3
4
5
6

Crossword:
1 down: d o l p h i n

2 Circle.

1  (These are) / This is crabs.

2 These are / This is a dolphin.

3 This is / These are a turtle.

4 These are / This is cameras.

22 There are lots of people.
Υπάρχουν πολλοί άνθρωποι.

22.01 **people** άνθρωποι
    person άνθρωπος
22.02 **men** άνδρες
    man άνδρας
22.03 **feed** ταΐζω
22.04 **women** γυναίκες
    woman γυναίκα

22.05 **tall** ψηλός, -ή, -ό
22.06 **shark** καρχαρίας
22.07 **teeth** δόντια
    tooth δόντι
22.08 **pool** πισίνα

box	boxes	fox	foxes
bus	buses	dress	dresses
watch	watches		
family	families	baby	babies
butterfly	butterflies	spy	spies
child	children	person	people
man	men	woman	women
foot	feet	tooth	teeth
fish	fish		

Όταν θέλουμε να μιλήσουμε για περισσότερα από ένα πρόσωπα, ζώα ή πράγματα, βάζουμε **-s** στο τέλος της λέξης (**apple** – **apples**).
Οι λέξεις, όμως, που τελειώνουν σε **-s** , **-x**, **-ch**, **-ss** παίρνουν την κατάληξη **-es** (**box** – **boxes**).
Εάν η λέξη τελειώνει σε σύμφωνο + **-y**, σβήνουμε το **-y** και βάζουμε **-ies** (**spy** – **spies**).
Τέλος, υπάρχουν και μερικές λέξεις που μεταμορφώνονται εντελώς (**child** – **children**)!

 1 Circle.

1 person / (people)

2 dolphin / shark

3 women / men

4 teeth / feet

23 There are some apples.
Υπάρχουν μερικά μήλα.

23.01 **bowl** μπωλ

23.02 **carrot** καρότο

23.03 **drawer** συρτάρι

23.04 **shelf** ράφι

23.05 **cherry** κεράσι

23.06 **sweets** καραμέλες

   sweet καραμέλα

23.07 **chocolate** σοκολάτα

23.08 **some** μερικοί, -ές, -ά

23.09 **bananas** μπανάνες

   banana μπανάνα

23.10 **But** Αλλά

23.11 **look for** ψάχνω

23.12 **secret store** μυστική κρυψώνα

23.13 **Are there any ...?**
   Υπάρχουν καθόλου ...;

23.14 **There aren't any ...**
   Δεν υπάρχουν καθόλου ...

23.15 **Yes, there are.** Ναι, υπάρχουν.

23.16 **No, there aren't.**
   Όχι, δεν υπάρχουν.

23.17 **toy box** κουτί με παιχνίδια

There is a cherry in the bowl.
Υπάρχει ένα κεράσι στο μπωλ.
There are some cherries in the bowl.
Υπάρχουν μερικά κεράσια στο μπωλ.
Are there any cherries in the bowl?
Υπάρχουν καθόλου κεράσια στο μπωλ;
There aren't any cherries in the bowl.
Δεν υπάρχουν καθόλου κεράσια στο μπωλ.

Όταν δε θέλουμε να μιλήσουμε για συγκεκριμένο αριθμό πραγμάτων, χρησιμοποιούμε τις λέξεις **some** (μερικοί, -ές, -ά) και **any** (καθόλου).
Το **some** το βάζουμε στην κατάφαση, ενώ στην ερώτηση και την άρνηση βάζουμε το **any**.

1 **Circle.**

1 There are some / any chocolates in the drawer.

2 There aren't some / any frogs in the river.

3 Are there some / any books in the bookcase?

4 There are some / any bananas on the shelf.

5 There aren't some / any sweets in the box.

6 Are there some / any toys in the toy box?

How many sweets are there?
Πόσες καραμέλες υπάρχουν;

24.01 **eleven** έντεκα

24.02 **twelve** δώδεκα

24.03 **thirteen** δεκατρία

24.04 **fourteen** δεκατέσσερα

24.05 **fifteen** δεκαπέντε

24.06 **sixteen** δεκαέξι

24.07 **seventeen** δεκαεφτά

24.08 **eighteen** δεκαοχτώ

24.09 **nineteen** δεκαεννιά

24.10 **twenty** είκοσι

24.11 **Who's coming?** Ποιος έρχεται;

24.12 **floor** πάτωμα

24.13 **singer** τραγουδιστής, τραγουδίστρια

Who is the winner? Ποιος είναι ο νικητής;
You are! Εσύ είσαι!
What are you doing? Τι κάνεις;
I'm hiding. Κρύβομαι.
Where are you hiding? Πού κρύβεσαι;
I'm hiding under the table.
Κρύβομαι κάτω από το τραπέζι.
How many friends have you got?
Πόσους φίλους έχεις;
I've got twenty friends! Έχω είκοσι φίλους!

Υπάρχουν κάποιες λέξεις που μπαίνουν στην αρχή της πρότασης και μας βοηθάνε να φτιάξουμε ερωτήσεις. Έτσι, όταν θέλουμε να ρωτήσουμε ποιος έκανε κάτι, χρησιμοποιούμε τη λέξη **Who** (Ποιος). Όταν ρωτάμε τι έκανε κάποιος, χρησιμοποιούμε τη λέξη **What** (Τι) και όταν ρωτάμε πού υπάρχει κάτι ή πού είναι κάποιος, τη λέξη **Where** (Πού). Τέλος, όταν ρωτάμε πόσα πράγματα υπάρχουν ή πόσα πράγματα έχει κάποιος, χρησιμοποιούμε τη φράση **How many** (Πόσοι, -ες, -α).

1 **Match.**

1 Where is Tag?
2 Who can swim?
3 What are they doing?
4 How many sweets are there?
5 Where are the sweets?

a In the bowl.
b They're playing basketball.
c Twenty.
d He's in the bedroom.
e Patty!

Tag's chart

Plurals

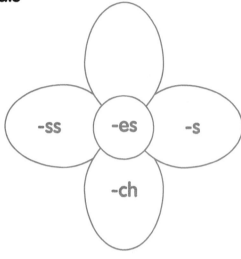

fox	fox**es**
bus	bus**es**
watch	watch**es**
dress	dress**es**

baby	bab**ies**
family	famil**ies**
butterfly	butterfl**ies**

Irregular plurals

child	children
man	men
woman	women
foot	feet
tooth	teeth
fish	fish

I've got two new watches. Look!

Sally's Story
Harry and Greta
Ο Χάρι και η Γκρέτα

SS.01 forest δάσος

SS.02 biscuit μπισκότο

SS.03 wall τοίχος

SS.04 little μικρός, -ή, -ό

SS.05 squirrel σκίουρος

SS.06 angry θυμωμένος, -η, -ο

SS.07 Good morning. Καλημέρα.

SS.08 come in έλα/ελάτε μέσα

SS.09 I've got you! Σ' έπιασα!

SS.10 Get in Μπες/Μπείτε μέσα

🐾 get in μπαίνω μέσα

SS.11 Stop it! Σταμάτα/Σταματήστε
(αυτό που κάνεις)!

🐾 stop σταματώ

Sally says ...

Όταν χρειαζόμαστε βοήθεια για οποιοδήποτε λόγο, λέμε απλά:

Help! Βοήθεια!

1 Write.

1 .... It's a wall. ....

2 ....

3 ....

4 ....

2 Find the odd one out.

1 (angry) trousers skirt

2 forest tree wall

3 little tall small

4 shark biscuit dolphin

5 squirrel door window

1 Choose and write.

chocolate   cherries   sweets   bowl   ~~kitchen~~   bananas

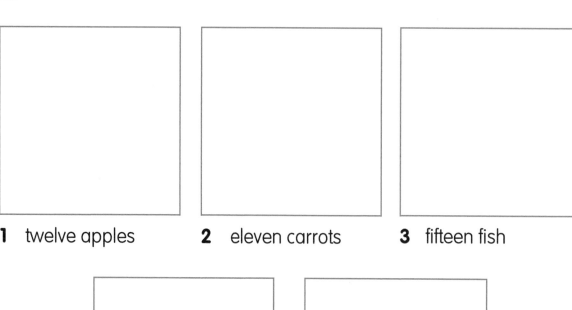

This is a (**1**) ....kitchen......... . Look at this big (**2**)

.... There are two (**3**) .... ,

twelve (**4**) .... and three (**5**) ....

Oh, no! There isn't any (**6**) ....

2 Draw and colour.

1 twelve apples   **2** eleven carrots   **3** fifteen fish

4 eighteen sweets   **5** twenty cherries

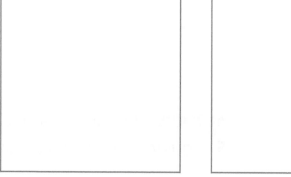

3 Write **This is** or **These are**.

1 .... This is .... a crab.

2 .... a turtle.

3 .... women.

4 .... sharks.

5 .... a biscuit.

4 Choose and write.

dress   foot   butterfly   ~~bus~~   fish

1 .... two buses ....

2 ....

3 ....

4 ....

5 ....

5 Write **some** or **any**.

1 There are ....some.... fish in the sea.

2 There aren't .... chocolates in the cupboard.

3 Are there .... pens in your bag?

4 There are .... toys in the toy box.

5 Are there .... squirrels in the forest?

25 I like breakfast.
Μου αρέσει το πρωινό.

25.01 **breakfast** πρωινό

25.02 **hungry** πεινασμένος, -η, -ο

25.03 **bread** ψωμί

25.04 **honey** μέλι

25.05 **milk** γάλα

25.06 **egg** αυγό

25.07 **orange** πορτοκάλι

25.08 **It's time** Είναι ώρα

25.09 **I like** μου αρέσει

25.10 **We like** Μας αρέσει

25.11 **You like** Σου αρέσει

25.12 **naughty** άτακτος, -η, -ο

25.13 **Here you are** Ορίστε

25.14 **morning** πρωί

25.15 **How about you?** Κι εσένα;

I like milk. Μου αρέσει το γάλα.
You like milk. Σου/Σας αρέσει το γάλα.
We like milk. Μας αρέσει το γάλα.
They like milk. Τους αρέσει το γάλα.

Όταν θέλουμε να πούμε τι μας αρέσει χρησιμοποιούμε το **like**.
Με τα **I**, **you**, **we**, **they**, όταν μιλάμε για πράγματα που κάνουμε συχνά ή κάθε μέρα, χρησιμοποιούμε το ρήμα όπως είναι.

1 Write.

1 ....milk.......

2 ....

3 ....

4 ....

5 ....

2 Write.

1 I ☺  ....I like red........

2 They ☺  ....

3 We ☺ ....

4 You ☺ ....

26 Do you like fish, Patty?
Σου αρέσει το ψάρι, Πάτι;

26.01 lunch μεσημεριανό φαγητό

26.02 pizza πίτσα

26.03 soup σούπα

26.04 chicken κοτόπουλο

26.05 salad σαλάτα

26.06 Do you like ...? Σου αρέσει ...;

Do you like pizza?   Yes, I do.

Σου αρέσει η πίτσα;   Ναι, μου αρέσει.

Do you like soup?   No, I don't.

Σου αρέσει η σούπα;   Όχι, δε μου αρέσει.

Do you play football in the morning?

Yes, I do./No, I don't.

Παίζεις ποδόσφαιρο το πρωί;

Ναι, (παίζω)./Όχι, (δεν παίζω).

Όταν θέλουμε να ρωτήσουμε κάποιον αν του αρέσει κάτι ή αν κάνει συχνά κάποια πράγματα, χρησιμοποιούμε τη βοηθητική λέξη **Do** στην αρχή της πρότασης. Χρησιμοποιούμε το **do** μόνο με τα **I, you, we**, και **they**. Απαντάμε σύντομα με **Yes**, το πρόσωπο και τη λέξη **do** ή με **No**, το πρόσωπο και τη λέξη **don't**.

 1 **Write.**

1 bread

2

3

4

5

2 **Write do or don't.**

1 Do you like breakfast?   Yes, I .... do ....

2 Do you like pizza?   No, I ....

3 Do you like lunch?   Yes, I ....

4 Do you like salad?   Yes, I ....

5 Do you like carrots?   No, I ....

27 He gets up at seven o'clock.
Σηκώνεται στις εφτά ακριβώς.

27.01 **get up** σηκώνομαι
(από το κρεβάτι)

27.02 **seven o'clock** επτά η ώρα
 o'clock ακριβώς
(όταν λέμε την ώρα)

27.03 **have breakfast**
τρώω πρωινό

27.04 **clean my teeth** καθαρίζω τα
δόντια μου

27.05 **go to school** πηγαίνω στο σχολείο

27.06 **every day** κάθε μέρα

27.07 **What's the time?** Τι ώρα είναι;

He reads books every morning.
(Αυτός) διαβάζει βιβλία κάθε πρωί.
She sees her friends every day.
(Αυτή) βλέπει τους φίλους της κάθε μέρα.

Με τα **he**, **she**, **it**, όταν μιλάμε για πράγματα που κάνουμε συχνά ή κάθε μέρα, βάζουμε **-s** στο τέλος του ρήματος.

 1 Choose and write.

come   get up   have   clean   ~~drink~~

1 It .... drinks .... milk every day.
2 She .... at eight o'clock.
3 She .... breakfast every morning.
4 He .... to the zoo every day.
5 He .... his teeth every morning.

2 Write.

1    **2**    **3**    **4**

1 He .... gets up .... every morning.
2 She .... every morning.
3 He .... every morning.
4 She .... every morning.

28 Does Rob go to the zoo every day?
Πηγαίνει ο Ρομπ στο ζωολογικό κήπο κάθε μέρα;

28.01 **Monday** Δευτέρα

28.02 **Tuesday** Τρίτη

28.03 **Wednesday** Τετάρτη

28.04 **Thursday** Πέμπτη

28.05 **Friday** Παρασκευή

28.06 **Saturday** Σάββατο

28.07 **Sunday** Κυριακή

28.08 **What day is it?** Τι μέρα είναι;

Does he eat bread every day?

Τρώει (αυτός) ψωμί κάθε μέρα;

Yes, he does. Ναι, (τρώει).

Does he drink milk every day?

Πίνει (αυτός) γάλα κάθε μέρα;

No, he doesn't. Όχι, (δεν πίνει).

Με τα **he, she it,** χρησιμοποιούμε τη βοηθητική λέξη **Does** και όχι το **Do** για να σχηματίσουμε την ερώτηση. Επίσης, δε βάζουμε **-s** στο ρήμα όπως είδαμε πριν. Απαντάμε σύντομα με **Yes**, το πρόσωπο και τη λέξη **does** ή με **No**, το πρόσωπο και τη λέξη **doesn't**.

 1 Find and circle. Then write.

A	H	N	U	S	B	S	T	J
M	O	N	D	A	Y	U	H	K
B	I	O	V	T	C	N	U	T
C	J	P	X	U	D	D	R	U
D	K	Q	U	R	E	A	S	E
E	F	R	I	D	A	Y	D	S
F	L	S	Z	A	F	I	A	D
G	M	T	A	Y	G	H	Y	A
W	E	D	N	E	S	D	A	Y

1 ..... Monday .....

2 .....

3 .....

4 .....

5 .....

6 .....

7 .....

Tag's chart

Present simple

I play tennis every day.
You play tennis every day.
He plays tennis every day.
She plays tennis every day.
It plays tennis every day.
We play tennis every day.
You play tennis every day.
They play tennis every day.

Do I play tennis every day?   Yes, you do./No, you don't.
Do you play tennis every day?   Yes, I do./No, I don't.
Does he play tennis every day?   Yes, he does./No, he doesn't.
Does she play tennis every day?   Yes, she does./No, she doesn't.
Does it play tennis every day?   Yes, it does./No, it doesn't.
Do we play tennis every day?   Yes, you do./No, you don't.
Do you play tennis every day?   Yes, we do./No, we don't.
Do they play tennis every day?   Yes, they do./No, they don't.

I clean my teeth every day.
Do you clean your teeth
every day?

Sally's Story
Superboy
Σούπερ-αγόρι

SS.01 **help** βοηθώ

SS.02 **police officer** αστυνομικός

SS.03 **fireman** πυροσβέστης

 firemen πυροσβέστες

SS.04 **visit** επισκέπτομαι

SS.05 **Superboy** σούπερ-αγόρι

SS.06 **week** εβδομάδα

SS.07 **old people** ηλικιωμένοι άνθρωποι

SS.08 **It's my pleasure.** Είναι ευχαρίστησή μου, Παρακαλώ.

SS.09 **Have a good day** Να έχεις/έχετε καλή μέρα

SS.10 **Well done** Πολύ καλά, Μπράβο

SS.11 **Don't mention it!** Δεν κάνει τίποτα!

SS.12 **I know.** Το ξέρω.

SS.13 **Help yourself** Σερβιρίσου

Sally says ...

Όταν κάποιος μας λέει 'ευχαριστώ' στα Αγγλικά, μπορούμε να απαντήσουμε με αρκετούς τρόπους. Μπορούμε να πούμε:
It's my pleasure.
Είναι ευχαρίστησή μου. ή
Don't mention it!
Δεν κάνει τίποτα!

1 Match.

1 dancer

2 teacher

3 clown

4 fireman

5 police officer

a

b

c

d

e

The Review 7

1 **Circle.**

ERTMONDAYUIOTUESDAYHJKWEDNESDAYDFGTHURSDAYZCVFRIDAYRTUSATURDAYBNKSUNDAYA

2 **Match.**

1 Thank you.
2 Here are the sweets. Help
3 Good morning.
4 How are you?
5 Good night.

a Fine, thank you.
b Sweet dreams.
c It's my pleasure.
d Have a good day.
e yourself.

3 **Choose and write.**

cherry   pizza   soup   ~~banana~~   chicken   orange

.........banana.........

....

....

....

....

4 **Read and answer.**

1 Does Ben like bananas?	Yes, he does.
2 Does Rachel like cherries?	
3 Do Ben and Rachel like milk?	
4 Does Rachel like chocolate?	
5 Does Ben like cherries?	

5 **Look and write.**

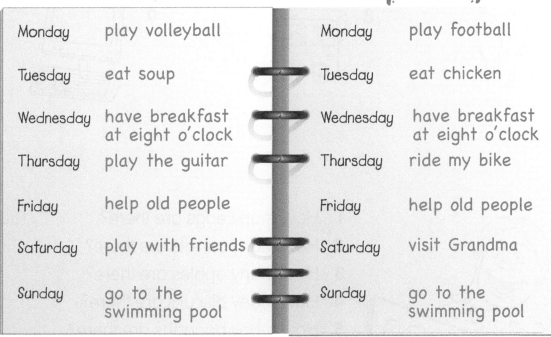

1 On Monday Superboy ___plays football___ .

2 On Tuesday Rob _____ .

3 On Wednesday Rob and Superboy _____ .

4 On Thursday Rob _____ .

5 On Friday Rob and Superboy _____ .

6 On Saturday Superboy _____ .

7 On Sunday Rob and Superboy _____ .

FUN AT YAZOO 3

1 **Colour.**

-s → blue   -es → red   -ies → green

1

2

3

4

5

6

7

8

9

2 **Write.**

1 How many eggs are there? ...... four ......
2 How many carrots are there? ....
3 How many apples are there? ....
4 How many biscuits are there? ....
5 How many bananas are there? ....

3 **Circle.**

1 (This is a forest.)/   **2** These are firemen.   **3** This is a watch. /
This is a   / These are police   This is a wall.
playground.   officers.

4 These are ghosts. /   **5** These are crabs. /
These are sharks.   These are fish.

4 **What about you? Write.**

1 Have you got any water pistols?   ....

2 Do you like pizza?   ....

3 Does your friend play basketball?   ....

4 Are there any books in your house?   ....

5 What's your favourite colour?   ....

Well done!

Happy Christmas!
Καλά Χριστούγεννα!

HC.01 **reindeer** τάρανδος

HC.02 **Christmas tree**
Χριστουγεννιάτικο δέντρο

HC.03 **star** αστέρι

HC.04 **Father Christmas** Αϊ-Βασίλης

HC.05 **ready** έτοιμος, -η, -ο

HC.06 **Ho, ho, ho.** Χο, χο, χο
(γέλιο του Αϊ-Βασίλη)

HC.07 **Christmas presents**
Χριστουγεννιάτικα δώρα

HC.08 **Jingle bells**
Οι καμπάνες κουδουνίζουν

HC.09 **Christmas Day**
Μέρα Χριστουγέννων

 1 Colour and write.

1	Christmas tree	**4**	
2		**5**	
3			

 2 Match and write.

1 bell

2

3

4

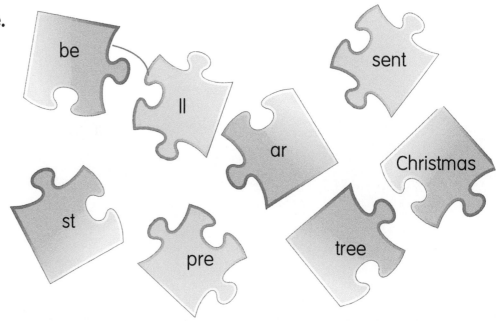

be

ll

sent

ar

Christmas

st

pre

tree

Happy Carnival!
Καλή Αποκριά!

HC.01 **throw** πετώ, ρίχνω

HC.02 **streamers** σερπαντίνες

 streamer σερπαντίνα

HC.03 **mask** μάσκα

HC.04 **dance** χορεύω

HC.05 **laugh** γελώ

HC.06 **Happy Carnival to you!**
Χαρούμενο Καρναβάλι
σε σένα/σας!

1 **Match.**

1 pirate

2 clown

3 cowboy

4 mask

5 streamers

a

b

c

d

e

2 **Find and write.**

1 skam ....mask........

2 srrteeasm ....

3 ulahg ....

4 aencd ....

5 whrot ....

Happy Easter!
Καλό Πάσχα!

HE.01 **Easter egg** Πασχαλινό αυγό

HE.02 **paint** βάφω

HE.03 **bunny** λαγουδάκι

HE.04 **Easter Bunny**

Πασχαλιάτικο λαγουδάκι

1 **Do the crossword.**

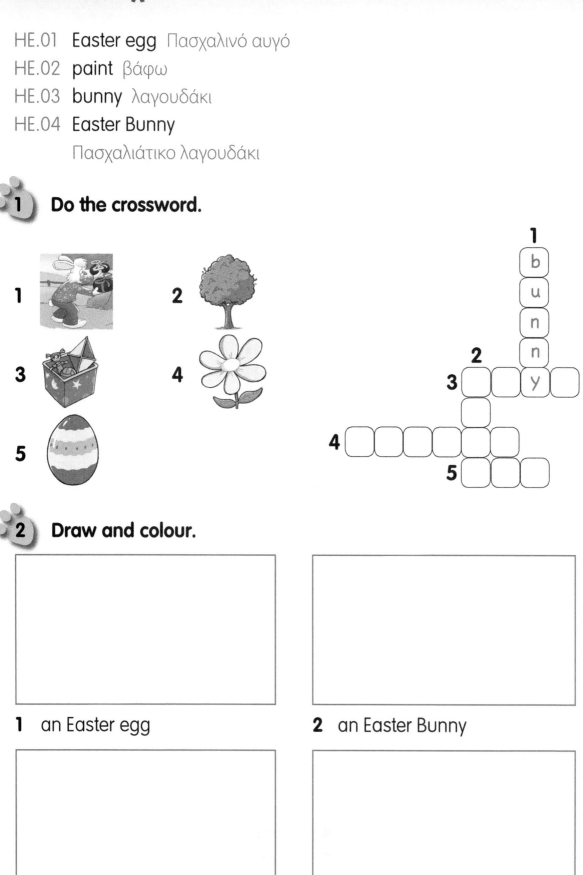

2 **Draw and colour.**

1 an Easter egg

2 an Easter Bunny

3 a flower

4 a tree

Pronunciation Guide
Οδηγός Προφοράς

Για να σας βοηθήσουμε να μάθετε πώς να προφέρετε σωστά τις αγγλικές λέξεις έχουμε φτιάξει ένα μικρό οδηγό προφοράς. Εδώ θα βρείτε την προφορά των λέξεων που πρέπει να ξέρετε γραμμένη με ελληνικά γράμματα, όπως επίσης και με μερικά ιδιαίτερα φωνητικά σύμβολα που αποδίδουν ήχους που δεν υπάρχουν στα Ελληνικά. Κοιτάξτε τη λίστα των συμβόλων που ακολουθεί, διαβάστε τα παραδείγματα και θα δείτε πόσο εύκολο είναι! Καλή σας επιτυχία!

æ   φωνήεν μεταξύ α και ε, όταν είναι υπογραμμισμένο **æ** σημαίνει ότι τονίζεται, π.χ. **and** ǽντ, **angry** ǽν(γκ)ρι

(χ)   ελαφρύ, απαλό χ όπως στη λέξη 'χαρά', π.χ. **hair** (χ)έəρ

ν(γκ) ελαφρύς, απαλός ήχος που συνήθως αποδίδει το **ng**, π.χ. **angry** ǽν(γκ)ρι

(γ)   ελαφρύς, απαλός ήχος που συνήθως αποδίδει τον ήχο του γράμματος **w**, π.χ. **away** ə(γ)ουέι

(τ)   προφέρεται απαλά, το **nt** /ν(τ)/ προφέρονται σα δύο ξεχωριστά γράμματα, π.χ. **Don't** ντόουν(τ)

μ(π) το **mp** προφέρονται σα δύο ξεχωριστά γράμματα, π.χ. **computer** κομ(π)ιούτəρ

ν(ντ) το ν και το ντ προφέρονται ξεχωριστά, π.χ. **friend** φρεν(ντ)

ə   προφέρεται σαν ένα πολύ ελαφρύ, ανεπαίσθητο ε το οποίο δεν τονίζεται ποτέ, π.χ. **about** əμπάουτ

s   παχύ σ, π.χ. **cherry** τséρι

z   παχύ ζ, π.χ. **pleasure** πλέzəρ

a   η υπογράμμιση σε φωνήεν δηλώνει ότι το φωνήεν είναι μακρό, π.χ. **arm** αρμ

/a/   πολύ κλειστό και σύντομο α, π.χ. **brother** μπρ/ά/δəρ

ρ   όταν είναι σε χρώμα σημαίνει ότι σχεδόν δεν προφέρεται, π.χ. **bear** μπέəρ

ə   όταν είναι σε χρώμα σημαίνει ότι σχεδόν δεν προφέρεται, π.χ. **apple** άπəλ

a ə (Welcome)
about əμπάουτ (5)
all ολ (11)
an əν (Welcome)
and æν(ντ) (Colours)
angry æν(γκ)ρι (SS p.97)
animal æνιμəλ (13)
animals æνιμəλζ (13)
apple æπəλ (Alphabet)
Are there any ...?
αρ δέəρ ένι (23)
Are they? αρ δέι (8)
Are we ...? αρ (γ)ουί (8)
Are you ...? αρ γιου (6)
arm αρμ (11)
Atishoo! ατσού (12)
away ə(γ)ουέι (17)
baby μπέιμπι (6)
bag μπæγκ (1)
ball μπολ (3)
balls μπολζ (3)
banana μπənάνə (23)
bananas μπənάνəζ (23)
basketball μπάσκετμπολ (19)
bathroom μπάθρουμ (SS p.83)
Be careful μπι κέəρφουλ (7)
be quiet μπι κουάιət (2)
bear μπέəρ (Alphabet)
beautiful μπιούτιφəλ (11)
bed μπεντ (SS p.71)
bedroom μπέντρουμ (SS p.83)
bicycle μπάισικəλ (9)
big μπιγκ (3, SS p.45)
bike μπάικ (9)
birthday μπέρθντέι (4)
biscuit μπίσκιτ (SS p.96)
black μπλæκ (Colours)
blue μπλου (Colours)
board μπορντ (2)
body μπόντι (11)
book μπουκ (1)
bookcase μπουκ κέις (SS p.71)
bowl μπόουλ (23)

box μποξ (7)
boy μπόι (6)
bread μπρεντ (25)
breakfast μπρέκφαστ (25)
brother μπρ/ά/δəρ (5)
brown μπράουν (Colours)
bunny μπ/ά/νι
(Happy Easter!)
bus μπ/α/ς (14)
But μπ/α/τ (23)
butterfly μπ/ά/τəρφλαϊ (12)
Bye bye μπάι μπάι (SS p.45)
cake κέικ (4)
camera κæμəρə (21)
can κæν (15)
Can you ...? κæν γιου (16)
car καρ (3)
card καρντ (3)
carrot κæρət (23)
carry κæρι (16)
cars καρζ (3)
cat κæτ (Alphabet)
chair τσέəρ (2)
cherry τσέρι (23)
chicken τσίκəν (26)
child τσάιλντ (13)
children τσίλντρəν (13)
chocolate τσόκλιτ (23)
Christmas Day κρίσμəς ντέι
(Happy Christmas!)
Christmas presents
κρίσμəς πρέζεντς
(Happy Christmas!)
Christmas tree
κρίσμəς τρι
(Happy Christmas!)
circus σέρκəς (SS p.58)
Clap κλæπ (5)
clean my teeth
κλιν μάι τιθ (27)
climb κλάιμ (15)
climbing frame
κλάιμιν(γκ) φρέιμ (14)

close κλόουζ (SS p.32)
clothes κλόουδζ (7)
clown κλάουν (8)
cockatoo κόκətου (13)
cockatoos κόκətουζ (13)
colour κ/ά/λəρ (Colours)
colours κ/ά/λəρζ (Colours)
cloudy κλάουντι (9)
come κ/α/μ (17)
Come back κ/α/μ μπæκ (9)
Come here κ/α/μ /χ/íəρ (3)
come in κ/α/μ ιν (SS p.96)
computer κομ(π)ιούτəρ
(SS p.71)
computer game
κομ(π)ιούτəρ γκέιμ (9)
cowboy κάουμποϊ (7)
crab κρæμπ (21)
crayon κρέιον (3)
crayons κρέιονζ (3)
crown κράουν (8)
cupboard κ/ά/πμπəρντ
(SS p. 70)
dad ντæντ (5)
dance ντæνς (5,
Happy Carnival!)
dancer ντæνσəρ (7)
desk ντεσκ (SS p.70)
do a handstand
ντου ə (χ)æν(ντ)στæν(ντ) (16)
do my homework
ντου μάι (χ)όουμ(γ)ερκ (17)
Do you like ...?
ντου γιου λάικ (26)
dog ντογκ (Alphabet)
doll ντολ (3)
dolls ντολζ (3)
dolphin ντόλφιν (21)
Don't mention it!
ντόουν(τ) μένσιəν ιτ (SS p.108)
door ντορ (SS p.32)
drawer ντρο (23)
dream ντριμ (20)

dress ντρες (18)
drink ντρινκ (20)
duck ντ/α/κ (SS p.44)
ear íəρ (12)
Easter Bunny íστəρ μπ/ά/νι
(Happy Easter!)
Easter egg íστəρ εγκ
(Happy Easter!)
eat ιτ (20)
egg εγκ (25)
eight έιτ (Numbers)
eighteen εϊτίν (24)
elephant έλεφαν(τ)
(Welcome)
eleven ιλέβən (24)
every day έβρι ντέι (27)
everyone έβριου/α/ν (16)
everywhere έβρι(γ)ουέə (12)
eye άι (12)
family φǽμəλι (5)
fantastic φαν(τ)ǽστικ (13)
fast φǽστ (10)
father φάδəρ (5)
Father Christmas
φάδəρ κρίσməς
(Happy Christmas!)
favourite φέιβəριτ (10)
feed φιντ (22)
feet φιτ (11)
fifteen φιφτίν (24)
fireman φάιρəмən (SS p.109)
fish φιs (21)
five φάιβ (Numbers)
floor φλορ (24)
flower φλάουəρ (Alphabet)
fly φλάι (16)
foot φουτ (11)
football φούτμπολ (19)
for φορ (Colours)
forest φόριστ (SS p.96)
four φορ (Numbers)
fourteen φορτίν (24)
fox φοξ (Alphabet)

Friday φράιντεϊ (28)
friend φρεν(ντ) (6)
frog φρογκ (SS p.32)
from φρομ (17)
funny φ/ά/νι (SS p.58)
Get in γκετ ιν (SS p.97)
get up γκετ /α/π (27)
ghost γκόουστ (SS p.83)
giant τzάιən(τ) (SS p.82)
girl γκερλ (6)
go γκəου (13)
go to school
γκəου του σκουλ (27)
goat γκəουτ (Alphabet)
gold γκəουλντ (8)
golden γκəουλντən (8)
Good morning.
γκουντ μόρνιν(γκ) (SS p.96)
Goodbye. γκουντμπάι
(Welcome)
Goodnight γκουντνάιτ
(SS p.83)
grandfather γκρǽντφαδəρ (6)
grandma γκρǽνμα (6)
grandmother
γκρǽνμ/α/δəρ (6)
grandpa γκρǽνπα (6)
green γκριν (Colours)
grey γκρέι (Colours)
ground γκράουν(ντ) (11)
Guess! γκιες (4)
hair (χ)έəρ (12)
hair slide (χ)έəρ σλάιντ (12)
hand (χ)æν(ντ) (7, 11)
hands (χ)æν(ντ)ζ (7)
happy (χ)ǽπι (7, SS p.44)
Happy Birthday
(χ)ǽπι μπέρθντεϊ (4)
Happy Carnival to you!
(χ)ǽπι κάρνιβəλ του γιου
(Happy Carnival!)
Has it got (χ)ǽζ ιτ γκοτ (12)
Have a good day

(χ)æβ ə γκουντ ντέι (SS p.108)
have a shower (χ)æβ ə
sάουəρ (18)
have breakfast
(χ)æβ μπρέκφαστ (27)
Have we got ...?
(χ)æβ (γ)ουί γκοτ (12)
He's (χ)ιζ (5)
head (χ)εντ (11)
hear (χ)íəρ (SS p.82)
Hello! (χ)έλοου (Welcome)
Help yourself
(χ)ελπ γιορσέλφ (SS p.109)
help (χ)ελπ (5, SS p. 108)
her (χ)ερ (9)
here χíəρ (10, 13)
Here (is, are) (χ)íəρ ιζ, αρ (10)
Here you are (χ)íəρ γιου αρ
(25)
Hi (χ)άι (Welcome)
hide (χ)άιντ (17)
high (χ)άι (15)
hippo (χ)íπ̌οου (Alphabet)
his (χ)ιζ (9)
Ho, ho, ho. (χ)óου (χ)óου
(χ)óου (Happy Christmas!)
honey (χ)/ά/νι (25)
Hooray! (χ)ουρέι (SS p.59)
hot (χ)οτ (14)
house (χ)άους (13)
How about you?
(χ)άου əμπάουτ γιου (25)
How are you? (χ)άου αρ
γιου (Welcome)
hungry (χ)/ά/ν(γκ)ρι (25)
I can't άι κæν(τ) (16)
I don't know.
άι ντον(τ) νόου (14)
I know άι νόου (SS p.109)
I love you άι λ/α/β γιου
(SS p. 45)
I'm ... άιμ (Welcome)
I'm fine άιμ φάιν (Welcome)

I've got άιβ γκοτ (11)
I've got you! άιβ γκοτ γιου (SS p.97)
I like άι λάικ (25)
idea αϊντία (SS p.71, 19)
in ιν (Welcome)
insect ίνσεκτ (Alphabet)
is ιζ (2)
Is he ...? ιζ χι (6)
Is she ...? ιζ **s**ι (6)
It's got ιτς γκοτ (11)
It's hot. ιτς (χ)οτ (14)
It's my pleasure.
ιτς μάι πλέ**z**əρ (SS p.108)
It's OK ιτς όου κέι (15)
It's sunny. ιτς σ/ά/νι (5)
It's time ιτς τάιμ (25)
It's ... ιτς (1)
its ιτς (9)
jelly **τz**έλι (Alphabet)
Jingle bells **τz**ιν(γκ)əλ μπελζ (Happy Christmas!)
jump **τz**/α/μ(π) (15)
kangaroo κ**æ**ν(γκ)əρου (Welcome)
keeper κί̱πəρ (Welcome)
king κιν(γκ) (8)
kitchen κί̱τ**s**əν (SS p.83)
kite κάιτ (9)
laugh λα̱φ (Happy Carnival!)
leg λεγκ (11)
Let's go λετς γκόου (7)
Let's learn
λετς λε̱ρν (Alphabet)
Let's race λετς ρέις (10)
lion λάιəν (Alphabet)
little λί̱τλ (SS p.97)
living room
λίβιν(γκ) ρουμ.
(SS p. 70, SS p.83)
long λον(γκ) (SS p.58)
look for λουκ φο̱ρ (23)
Lots of λοτς οβ (3)
love λ/α/β (Welcome)

lovely λ/ά/βλι (4)
lucky λ/ά/κι (11)
lunch λ/α/ντ**s** (26)
man μ**æ**ν (22)
mask μ**æ**σκ (Happy Carnival!)
me μι (3)
men μεν (22)
milk μιλκ (25)
mobile phone
μόουμπάιλ φόουν (SS p.71)
Monday μ/ά/ν(ντ)έϊ (28)
monkey μ/ά/νκι (Welcome)
morning μόρνιν(γκ) (25)
mother μ/ά/δəρ (5)
mouth μάουθ (12)
mum μ/α/μ (5)
my μάι (1)
My name's ...
μάι νέιμς (Welcome)
naughty νότι (25)
nest νεστ (Alphabet)
new νιου (9)
next to νεξτ του (14)
nine νάιν (Numbers)
nineteen ναϊντί̱ν (24)
No. νόου (2)
No, he isn't. νόου χι ιζν(τ) (6)
No, I haven't.
νόου άι (χ)**æ**βəν(τ) (12)
No, I'm not. νόου άιμ νοτ (6)
No, there aren't.
νόου δέəρ α̱ρəν(τ) (23)
No, we haven't.
νόου (γ)ουί (χ)**æ**βəν(τ) (12)
noise νόι**z** (20)
nose νόου**z** (12)
now νάου (11)
number ν/ά/μπəρ
(Numbers)
numbers ν/ά/μπəρ**z**
(Numbers)
o'clock οκλόκ (27)
octopus όκτəπους (Alphabet)
Oh, dear! όου ντίəρ (11)

old όουλντ (9)
old people όουλντ πι̱πəλ
(SS p. 108)
on ον (2)
one ου/ά/ν (Numbers)
open όουπəν
(SS p. 33)
orange όριντ**z** (Colours, 25)
our άουəρ (10)
paint πέιν(τ) (Happy Easter!)
park πα̱ρκ (13)
pen πεν (1)
pencil πένσιλ (1)
penguin
πέν(γκ)ουιν (Welcome)
people πί̱πəλ (22)
person πέ̱ρσəν (22)
pet πετ (11)
picture πίκτ**s**ə (20)
pink πινκ (Colours)
pirate πάιρəτ (8)
pizza πί̱τσα (26)
play πλέι (17)
play the guitar
πλέι δə γκιτά̱ρ (15)
playground
πλέιγκραουν(ντ) (13)
please πλι̱ζ (2)
police officer
πəλίς όφισəρ (SS p.108)
pool που̱λ (22)
present πρέ**z**εν(τ) (4)
pretty πρί̱τι (5)
prize πράι**z** (10)
purple πέ̱ρπəλ (Colours)
queen κουί̱ν (Alphabet)
Quick! κουίκ (12)
rabbit ρ**æ**μπιτ (Alphabet)
radio ρέιντιοου (9)
raining ρέινιν(γκ) (21)
read ρι̱ντ (17)
ready ρέντι
(Happy Christmas!)
red ρεντ (Colours)

reindeer ρέιν(ντ)ιəρ
(Happy Christmas!)
ride ράιντ (15)
river ρίβəρ (13)
roar ρο̲ρ (20)
robot ρόουμποτ (4)
rollerblade
ρόουλəμπλεϊντ (10, 16)
rollerblades
ρόουλəμπλεϊντζ (10)
rubber ρ/ά/μπəρ (1)
run ρ/α/ν (16)
sad σæντ (SS p.45)
salad σæ̲λəντ (26)
Saturday σæ̲τəρντεϊ (28)
says σεζ (SS p.83)
school σκο̲υλ (1)
sea σι̲ (15)
secret store σίκρετ στο̲ρ (23)
see σι̲ (8)
seven σέβəν (Numbers)
seven o'clock σέβəν
οκλόκ (27)
seventeen σεβə(ν)τί̲ν (24)
shark **s**α̲ρκ (22)
she's **s**ι̲ζ (5)
She's got **s**ι̲ζ γκοτ (11)
shelf **s**ελφ (23)
shoe **s**ου (18)
shoes **s**ουζ (18)
shop **s**οπ (14)
short **s**ορτ (SS p.59)
sing σίν(γκ) (15)
singer σίν(γκ)əρ (24)
sister σίστəρ (5)
sit down σιτ ντάουν
(SS p. 33)
six σιξ (Numbers)
sixteen σιξτί̲ν (24)
skip σκιπ (16)
skirt σκε̲ρτ (18)
sky σκάι (15)
sleep σλι̲π (17)

slide σλάιντ (14)
slow σλόου (10)
small σμολ (SS p.45)
snake σνέικ (Alphabet)
snore σνο̲ρ (20)
some σ/α/μ (23)
Sorry σόρι (5)
soup σουπ (26)
spell σπελ (2)
splash σπλæ**s** (19)
spy σπάι (7)
squirrel σκουίρəλ (SS p.97)
Stamp στæμ(π) (11)
stand up! στæν(ντ) /α/π
(SS p.33)
star στα̲ρ
(SS p.59, Happy Christmas!)
sticker στίκəρ (3)
stickers στίκəρζ (3)
stop στοπ (SS p.97)
Stop it! στοπ ιτ (SS p.97)
streamer στρί̲μəρ
(Happy Carnival!)
streamers στρί̲μəρζ
(Happy Carnival!)
strong στρον(γκ) (SS p.59)
Sunday σ/ά/ν(ντ)εϊ (28)
sunny σ/ά/νι (5)
Superboy σούπəμπόϊ
(SS p.108)
swan σουόν (SS p.45)
sweater σουέτəρ (18)
sweets σουίτς (23)
sweet σουίτ (23)
Sweet dreams
σουίτ ντρι̲μζ (SS p.83)
swim σουίμ (15)
swimming pool
σουίμιν(γκ) πουλ (13)
swing σουίν(γκ) (14)
table τέιμπəλ (SS p.71)
take a photo
τέικ ə φόουτο (21)
tall το̲λ (22)

teacher τι̲τ**s**əρ (SS p. 32)
teeth τι̲θ (22)
ten τεν (Numbers)
tennis τένις (19)
terrible τέριμπəλ (9)
thank you θένκιου (Welcome)
That is δæτ ιζ (4)
That's δæτς (4)
that's terrible
δæτς τέριμπəλ (15)
the δə (Welcome)
their δέəρ (10)
then δεν (11)
There are δέəρ α̲ρ (13)
There aren't any
δέəρ αρəν'(τ) ένι (23)
There isn't δέəρ ίζəν(τ) (14)
There's δέəρζ (13)
These are δι̲ζ α̲ρ (21)
They're ... δέəρ (3)
They've got δέιβ γκοτ (11)
thing θιν(γκ) (16)
things θιν(γκ)ζ (16)
thirteen θερτί̲ν (24)
This is ... δις ιζ (4)
three θρι̲ (Numbers)
throw θρόου
(Happy Carnival!)
Thursday θέρζντεϊ (28)
tiger τάιγκəρ (Welcome)
tired τάιρəντ (19)
to the beat του δə μπιτ (11)
toast τόουστ (SS p.83)
today τουντέι (7)
too το̲υ (Colours)
tooth το̲υθ (22)
touch τ/α/τ**s** (11)
town τάουν (13)
toy τόι (10)
toy box τόι μποξ (23)
toys τόιζ (10)
train τρέιν (10)
tree τρι̲ (13)

treehouse τρί(χ)αους (14)

trousers τράουζəρς (SS p.18)

trunk τρ/α/νκ (SS p.59)

T-shirt τι sερτ (18)

Tuesday τιούζντεϊ (28)

turn around
τερν əράουν(ντ) (11)

turtle τέρτλ (21)

twelve τουέλβ (24)

twenty τουέντι (24)

two του (Numbers)

umbrella /α/μπρέλα
(Alphabet)

under /ά/ν(ντ)əρ (14)

upstairs /ά/πστεəρζ (20)

us /α/σ (20)

very βέρι (SS p.58)

Very good βέρι γκουντ (2)

visit βίζιτ (SS p.109)

volleyball βόλεϊμπολ (19)

vulture β/ά/λτsəρ (Alphabet)

walk (γ)ουόκ (16)

wall (γ)ουόλ/ (SS p.97)

watch (γ)ουότs (4)

water pistol
(γ)ουότəρ πίστəλ (17)

we (γ)ουί (Welcome)

We can't (γ)ουί κæν(τ) (16)

We like (γ)ουί λάικ (25)

We're (γ)ουίρ (7)

We've got (γ)ουίβ γκοτ (11)

wear (γ)ουέəρ (18)

Wednesday (γ)ουένζντεϊ (28)

week (γ)ουίκ (SS p.108)

Well done (γ)ουέλ ντ/α/ν
(SS p.108)

whale (γ)ουέιλ (Alphabet)

What a mess! (γ)ουότ ə μες (9)

What are these?
(γ)ουότ αρ διζ (21)

What are they doing?
(γ)ουότ αρ δέι ντούιν(γκ) (20)

What are they?

(γ)ουότ αρ δέι (3)

What are we?

(γ)ουότ αρ (γ)ουί (8)

What day is it?

(γ)ουότ ντέι ιζ ιτ (28)

What's that? (γ)ουότς δæτ
(SS p.33)

What's the matter?

(γ)ουότς δə μæτəρ (SS p.70)

What's the time?

(γ)ουότς δə τάιμ (27)

What's this? (γ)ουότς δις (1)

What's your name?

(γ)ουότς γιόρ νέιμ (Welcome)

What's your number?

(γ)ουότς γιορ ν/ά/μπəρ (SS
p.71)

Where are ...?

(γ)ουέəρ αρ (14)

Where's (γ)ουέρζ (14)

white (γ)ουάιτ (Colours)

Who's coming?

(χ)ουζ κ/ά/μιν(γκ) 24

window (γ)ουίν(ντ)οου
(SS p.33)

wing (γ)ουίν(γκ) (11)

winner (γ)ουίνəρ (10)

with (γ)ουίδ (5)

woman (γ)ούμəν (22)

women (γ)ουίμιν (22)

Wow! (γ)ουάου (7)

write ράιτ (2)

yellow γέλοου (Colours)

Yes. γες (2)

Yes, it has. γες ιτ (χ)æζ (12)

Yes, of course.
γες əφ κορς (21)

Yes, she is. γες si ιζ (6)

Yes, there are.
γες δέəρ αρ (23)

you γιου (Colours)

You like γιου λάικ (25)

your γιορ (4)

yo-yo γιόου γιόου (Alphabet)

zebra ζέμπρə (Alphabet)

zoo ζου (Welcome)